Excel Create and Learn Dashboard using PivotTable Second Edition

Roger F. Silva

Copyright © 2017 by Roger F. Silva

All rights reserved. No part of this publication may be reproduced, distributed, or transmitted in any form or by any means, including photocopying, recording, or other electronic or mechanical methods, without the prior written permission of the publisher, except in the case of brief quotations embodied in critical reviews and certain other non-commercial uses permitted by copyright law. For permission requests, write to the publisher, addressed "Attention: Permissions Coordinator," at the address below.

Roger F. Silva

rogerfsilva01@gmail.com

rogerfsilva.blogspot.com

Table of Contents

1. Introduction 4
2. Downloading the files 8
3. Exercise 1: Line Chart "Sales by Season" 9
4. Exercise 2: Doughnut Chart "Smartphone Users". 19
5. Exercise 3: Funnel Chart "Sales Pipeline". 28
6. Exercise 4: Bar Chart "Customer Satisfaction" 34
7. Sales Dashboard 48
    1. Data Formatting 49
    2. Working with formulas 58
    3. Creating PivotTables 63
    4. Creating PivotCharts 73
    5. Slicers and Timeline 94
    6. Doughnut Charts and Links 101
    7. Aligning Charts and objects 109
    8. Printing setup 112
    9. Training tab 117

1. Introduction

Dear Reader,

I have used Microsoft Excel professionally for more than 15 years, teaching and working in multinational companies.

During this period, hundreds of people came to me for help, asked questions and complained about how difficult it was to learn Excel. Whilst looking further into the matter, I observed that the courses and books available were very long, tiring and expensive. People had difficulty learning the "Real-World Excel."

This book was designed to teach you how to build a beautiful Dashboard using PivotTables, slicers, timeline, print setup, and more.

Also, you will have the chance to create four beautiful customized charts through the exercises in the beginning of the book, and a training Dashboard. I will not go into deep theories as the purpose of this book is to Create and Learn.

You will follow step-by-step instructions on the creation of a Dashboard, and several customized infographics, rapidly increasing your knowledge.

If you want to expand your knowledge of the wonderful tool that is Ms Excel, check out my other publications that are focused on market needs and fast learning.

Thank you for Creating and Learning.

Roger F. Silva

rogerfsilva01@gmail.com

rogerfsilva.blogspot.com

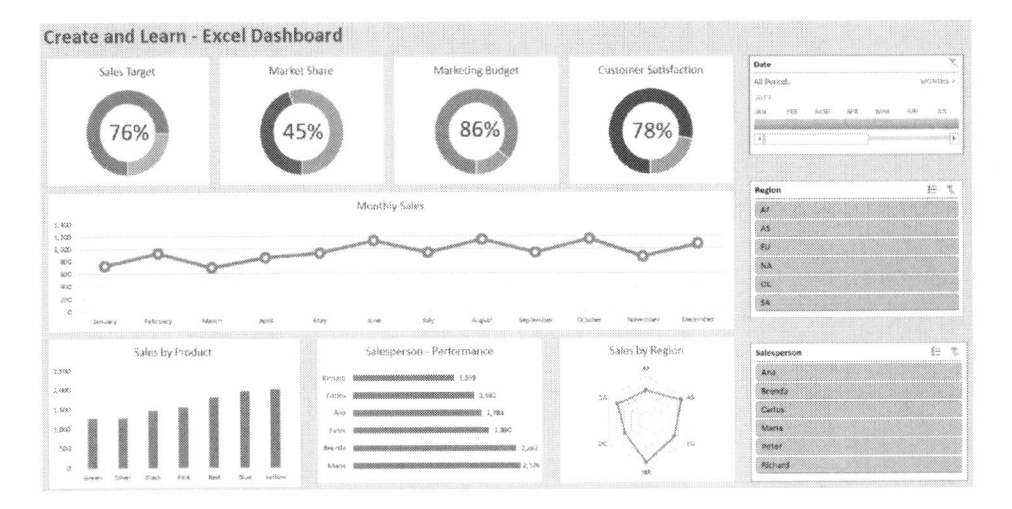

Book subject: Dashboard using PivotTable

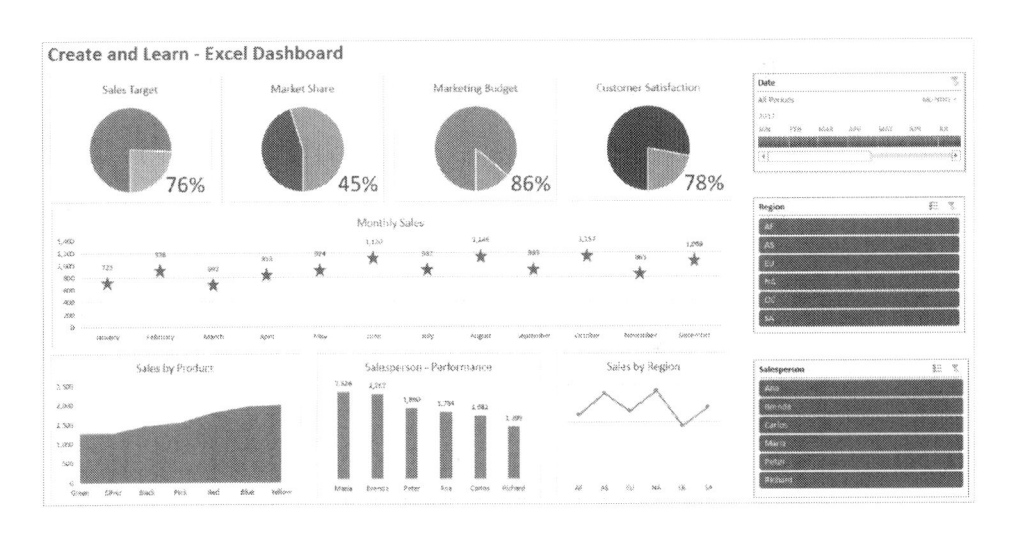

Training Dashboard

Exercise 1: Line Chart "Sales by Season".

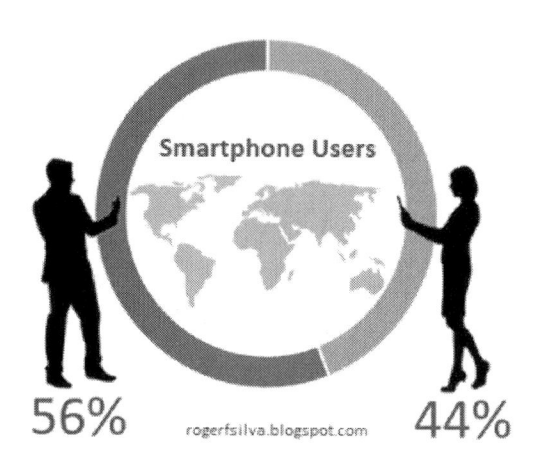

Exercise 2: Doughnut Chart "Smartphone Users"

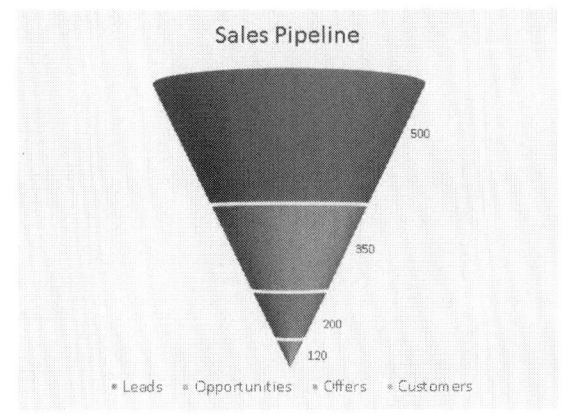

Exercise 3: Funnel Chart "Sales Pipeline"

Exercise 4: Bar Chart "Customer Satisfaction"

2. Downloading the files

You can download the images that will be used in the exercises, and the database table to be used with the Dashboard. If you don't want to use the file with the Dashboard data, there is no problem, you can type the content that is available in the Dashboard chapter.

To Download the content, go to:

http://rogerfsilva.blogspot.com/2017/06/books.html

There, you will be able to download the excel file and images.

3. Exercise 1: Line Chart "Sales by Season"

In this warm-up exercise you will be able to create a customized line chart work with images and intermediate level chart configuration.

1- Create a new file and type Jan in cell A1. You will save your time by using the "Auto Fill" feature. In cell A1 move your mouse to the little handle in the bottom-right corner, the mouse handle will turn into a black cross (see picture below).

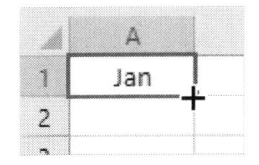

2- Click and drag until L1 to use the "Auto Fill" feature.

3- Type the values in figure below.

	A	B	C	D	E	F	G	H	I	J	K	L
1	Jan	Feb	Mar	Apr	May	Jun	Jul	Aug	Sep	Oct	Nov	Dec
2	60	50	60	70	80	95	110	120	100	80	75	70

4- Select Range A1:L2. Go to "Home" tab, "Borders" and "All borders.

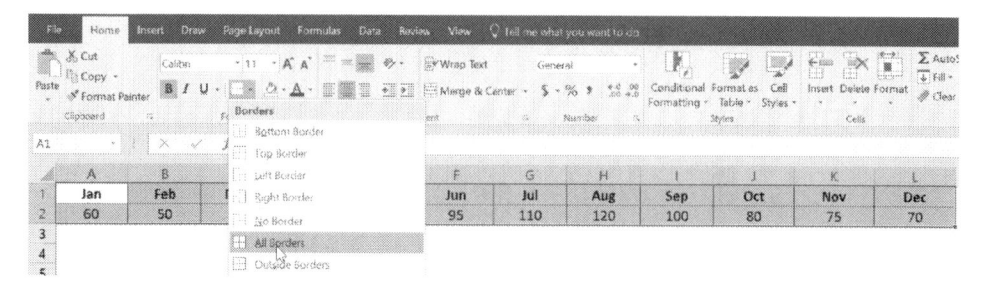

5- Go to "Page Layout'" tab, "Sheet Options" and deselect Gridlines View.

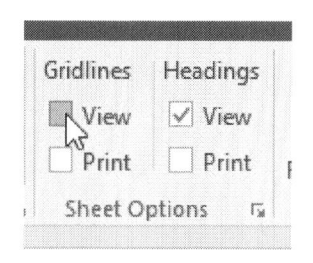

6- Go to "Insert" tab, "Charts" group, "Insert Line Chart" and select "Line with Markers".

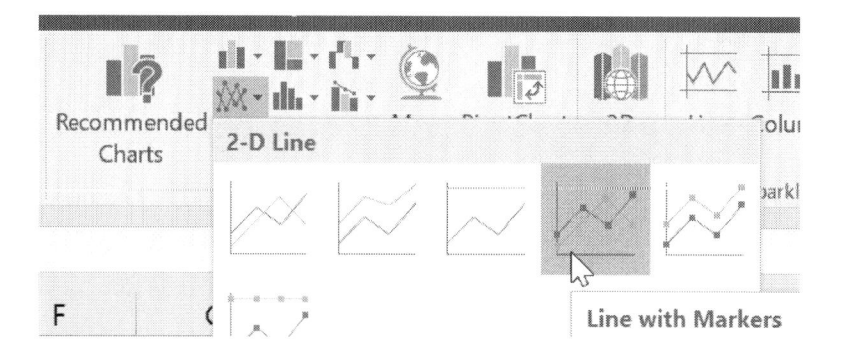

7- Right click the Vertical axis on the chart and select "Format Axis".

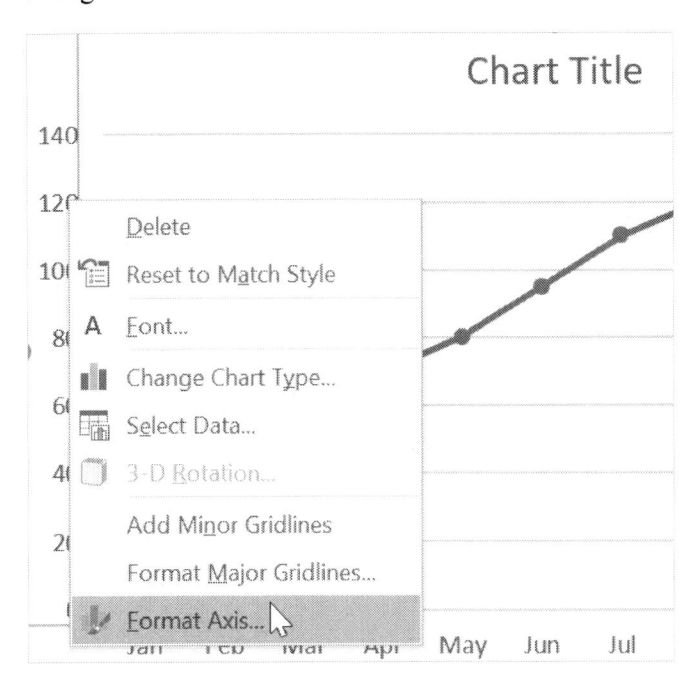

8- Go to "Axis Options", "Bounds" and type Minimum 0 and Maximum 200.

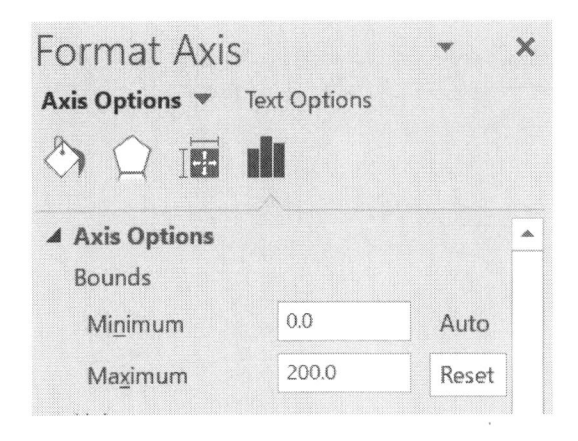

9- Select chart. Go to "Chart Elements", "Gridlines" and check only "Primary major Vertical".

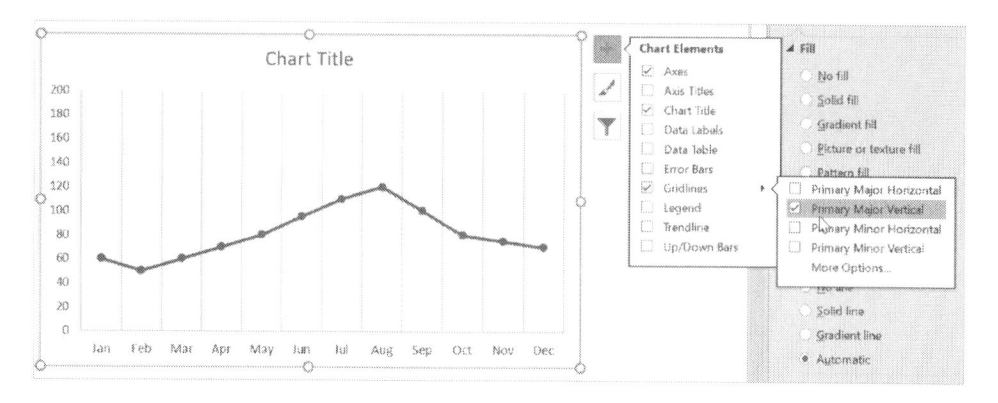

10- Right Click the Horizontal Axis. Go to "Format Axis", "Axis Options", "Tick Marks", "Interval Between Marks" and type **3**.

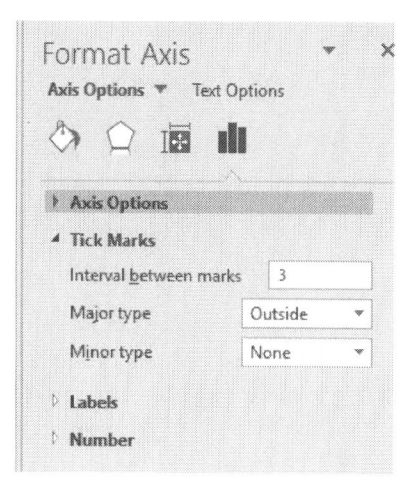

11- Go to "Chart Elements" and Deselect "Axes" or just select axes and press "Delete" key.

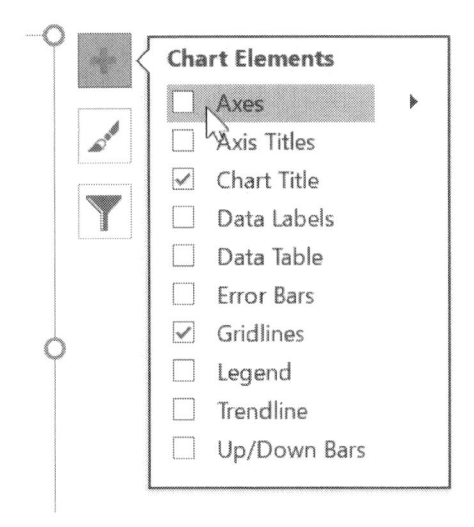

12 - Right click the Chart Series (blue line in the chart) and select "Format Data Series". Go to "Fill & Line", select "Markers" and set as Figure below.

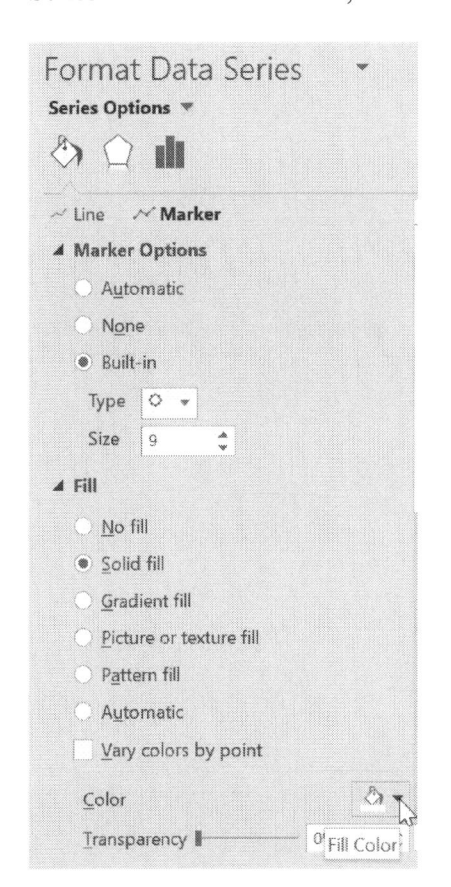

13- Border Color will be "Light Grey, Background 2, Darker 75%" and "Width" 3.25 pt.

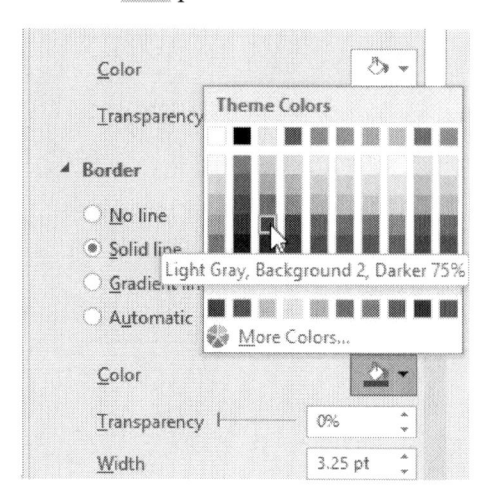

14- Go to Line change the Color to " Light Grey, Background 2, Darker 75%" and "Width" 3.25 pt.

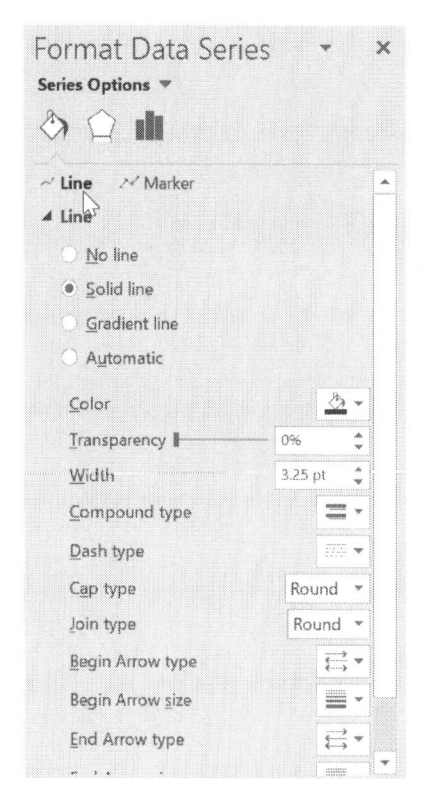

15- Select Axis Major Gridlines and go to "Format Major Gridline", "Line" change color to light gray, width to 1.5 pt and "Dash Type" to Dash.

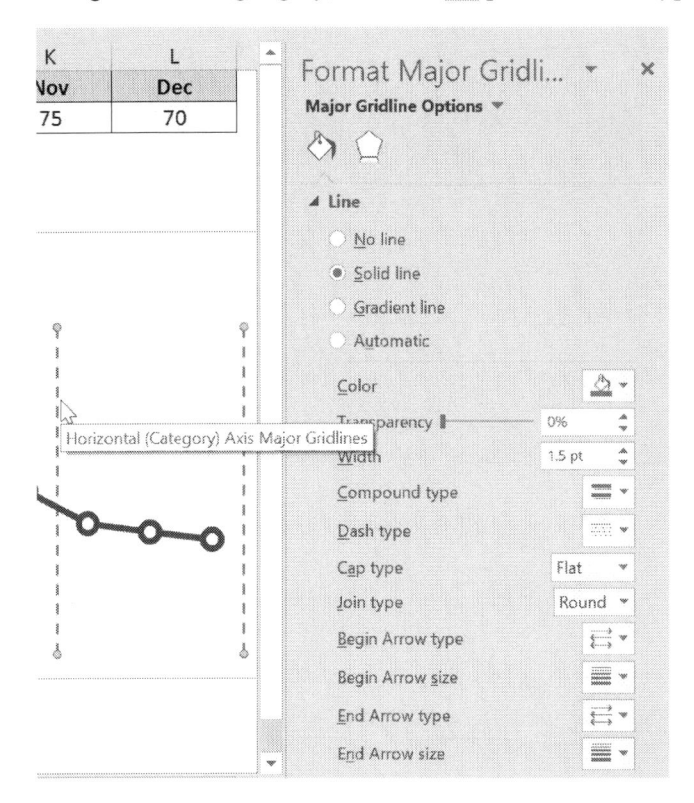

16- Go to the link below and save the five images below by right clicking the image and selecting "Save image as"

http://rogerfsilva.blogspot.com/2017/06/books.html

17- Go to "Insert" tab, "Illustrations" group, click in "Picture" and choose the images that you just saved.

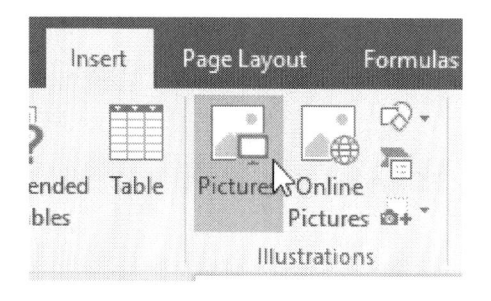

18- For the seasons icons. Go to "Format" tab, "Size" group and set "Height" 1.5 cm.

19- The Sunglasses picture will have "Height" 3.5 cm

20- Select, click and drag the figures to the position as same as figure below.

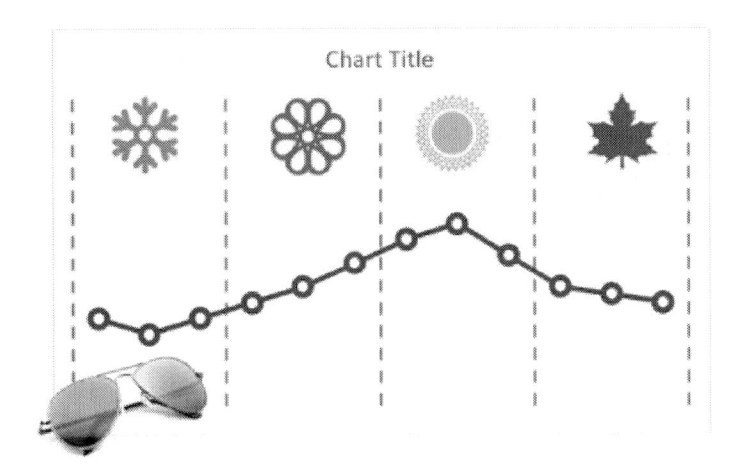

21- Select Chart. Go to "Format Tab", "Shape Styles Group", "Shape Outline" and select "No Outline".

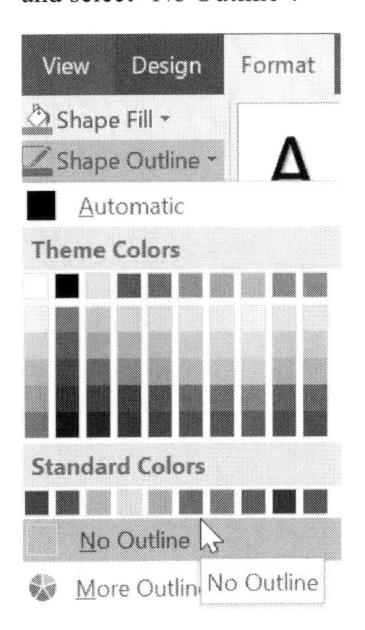

22- At Chart Title, type SALES BY SEASON.

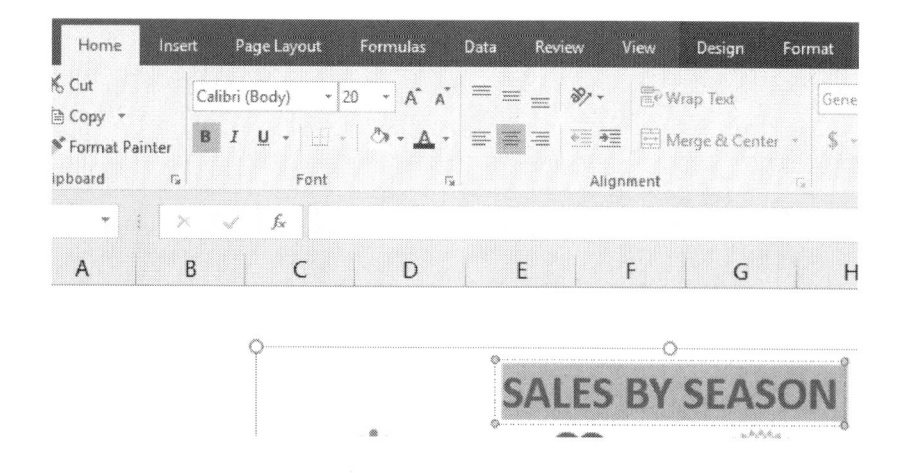

23- Congratulations! You have created a Customized Chart by using advance configuration and figures.

4. Exercise 2: Doughnut Chart "Smartphone Users".

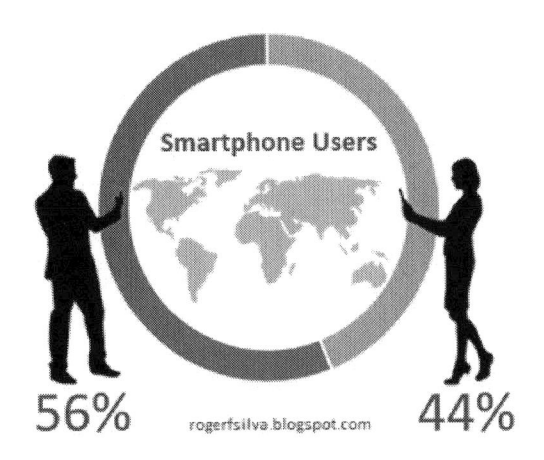

Infographics are great communication tools and have been used through every media available. You can create beautiful Infographics in Excel. In this warm-up exercise you will create a customized doughnut chart and will work with links.

1- Type the words and numbers in Range A1:B2.

	A	B
1	Woman	44%
2	Man	56%
3		

2- Go to "Page Layout'" tab, "Sheet Options" and deselect Gridlines View.

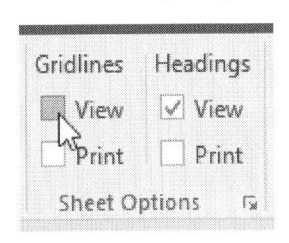

3- Select Range A1:B2. Go to "Insert" tab, "Charts" group and select "Doughnut"

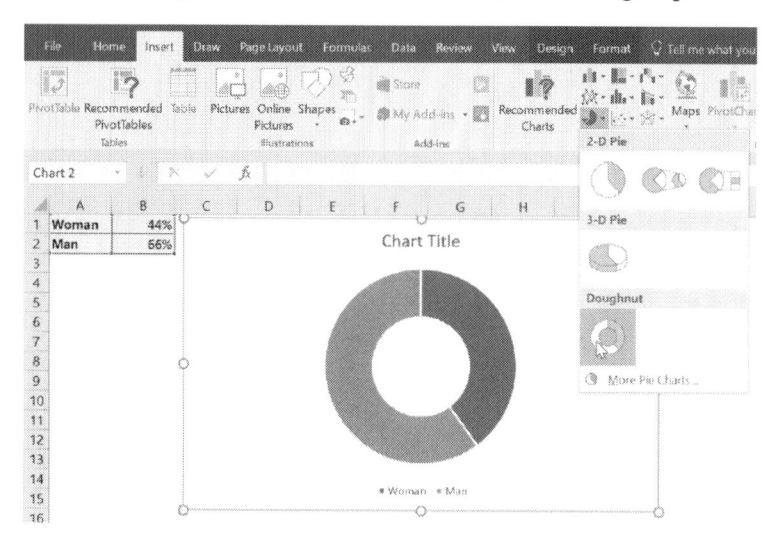

4- Select Legend and press 'Delete" key.

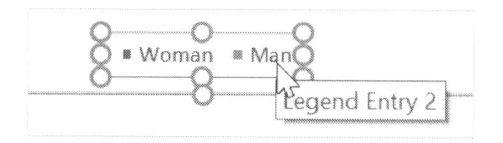

5- Select Chart Title and press "Delete" key

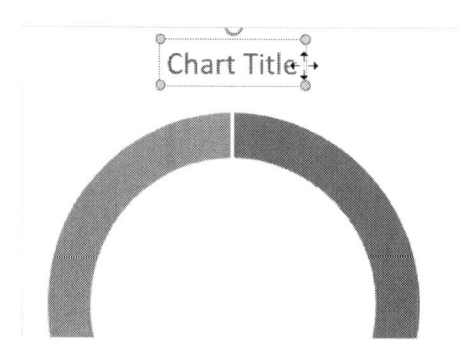

6- Select the chart. Go to "Format" tab, "Shape Fill" and select "No Fill". Go to "Shape Outline" and select "No Outline".

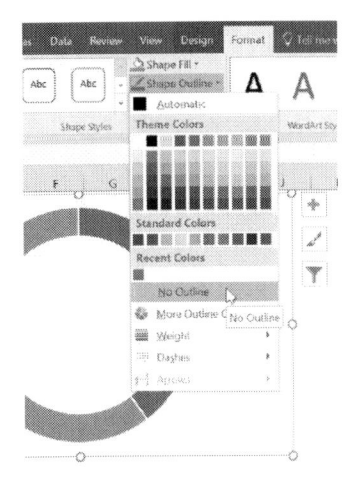

7- Double-click the series "Woman".

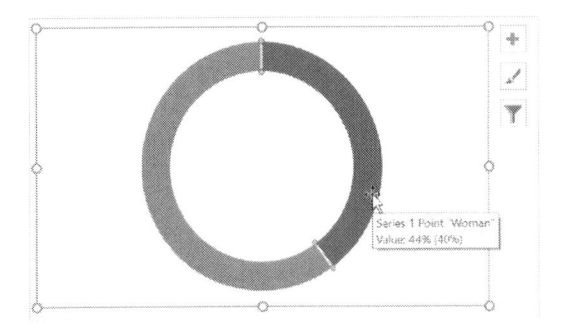

8- Go to "Format" tab, 'Shape Fill", "More Fill Colors" and select Pink color.

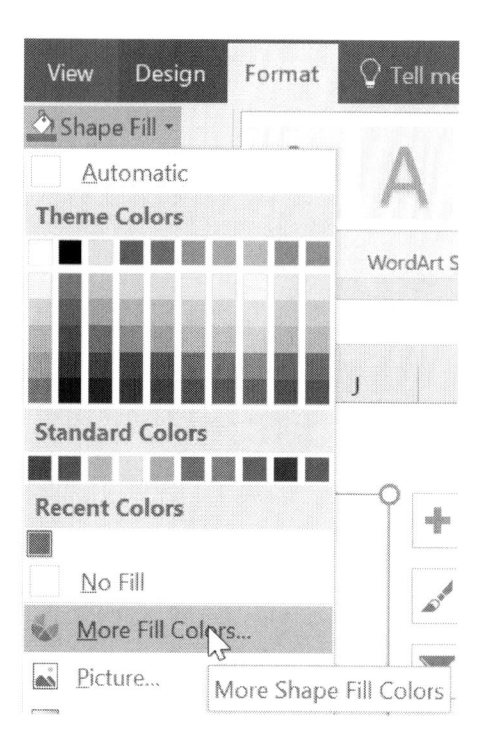

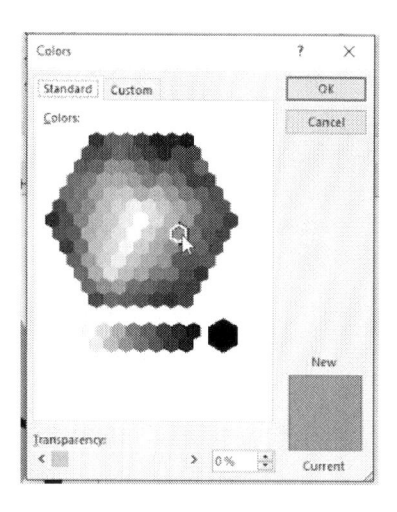

9- Double-Click the series "Man" and select color "Blue, Accent 1, Darker 25%".

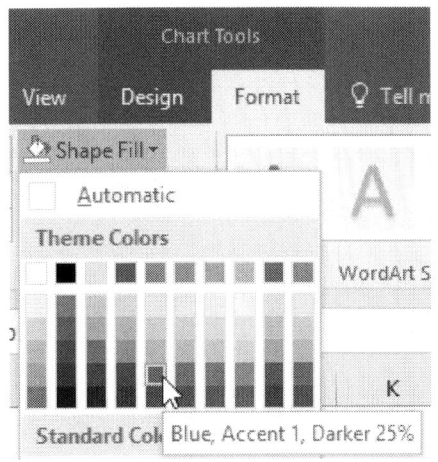

10- With the series selected go to "Format Data Point", "Series Options" and type 81% in Doughnut Hole Size.

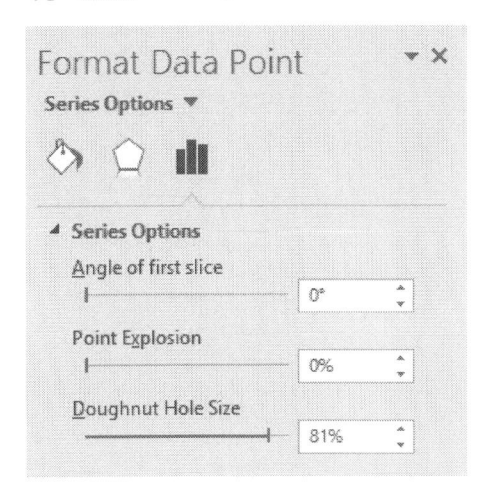

11- Go to "Insert" tab, "Text" group and click on "Text Box".

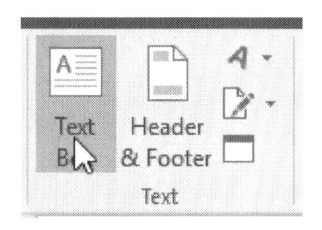

12- Click and drag to draw a Text Box. With the text box selected type in Formula Bar =B1 to link the B1 value into the text box.

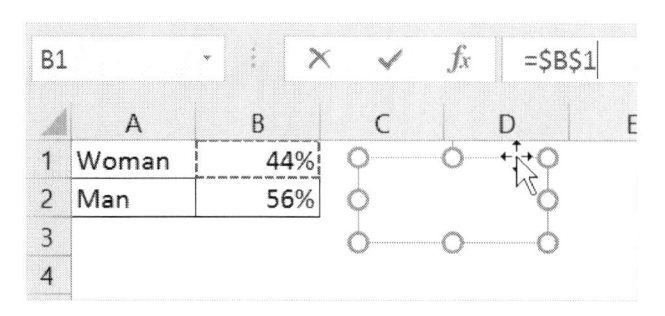

13- Insert a new text box and with it selected type =B2 in the Formula Bar.

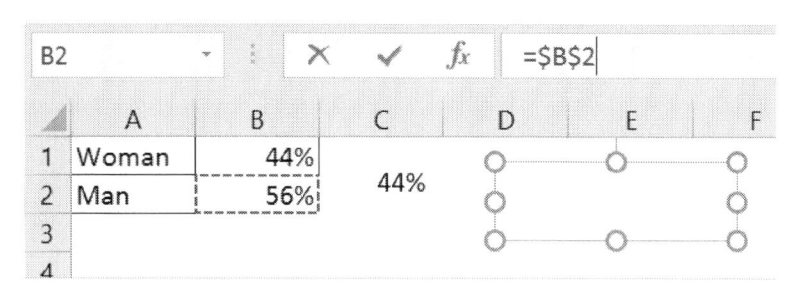

14- Select the text boxes and configure them to "Calibri Font", "Size 32", "Center", "No Shape Outline" and "Black, Text 1, Lighter 25%" color.

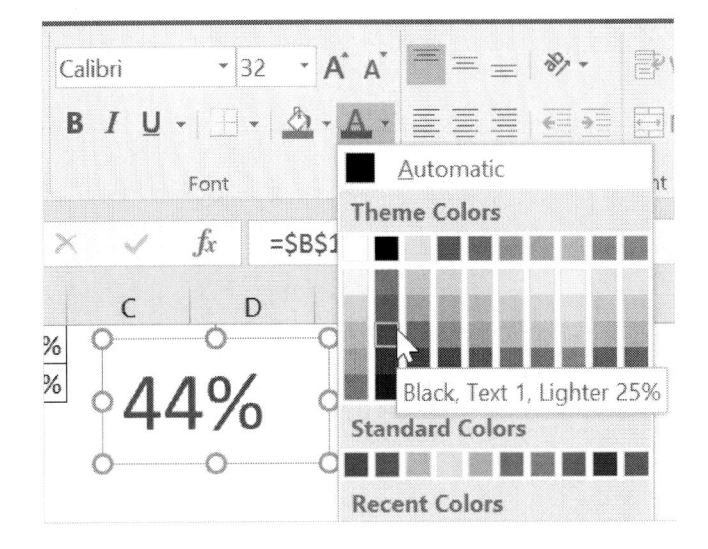

15- Click and drag the text boxes to the bottom.

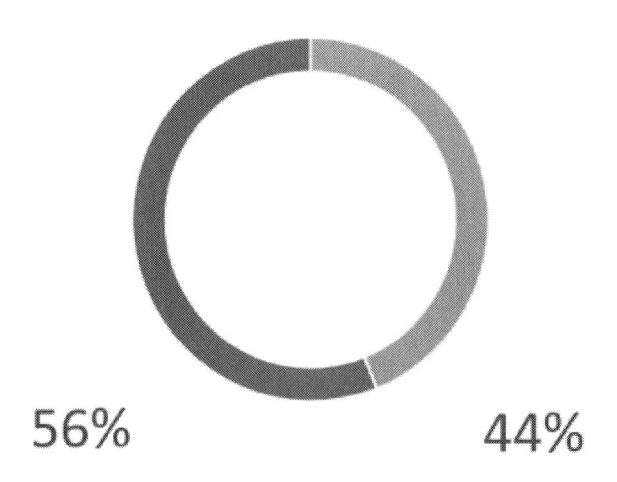

16- Go to the link below and save the 3 images below (Men, Woman and World Map) by right clicking the image and selecting "Save image as".

http://rogerfsilva.blogspot.com/2017/06/books.html

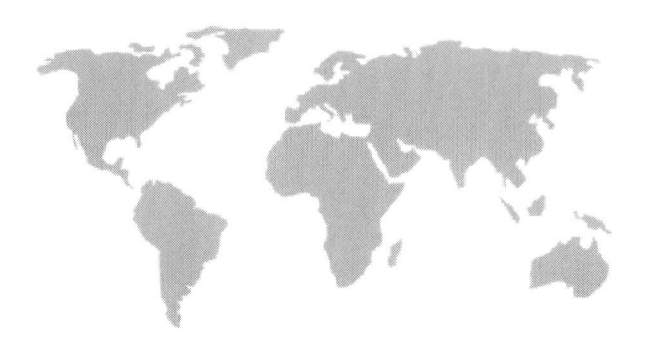

17- Go to "Insert" tab, "Illustrations" group, click in "Picture" and select the images that you just saved.

18- Click, drag the images and re-size them as show in figure below.

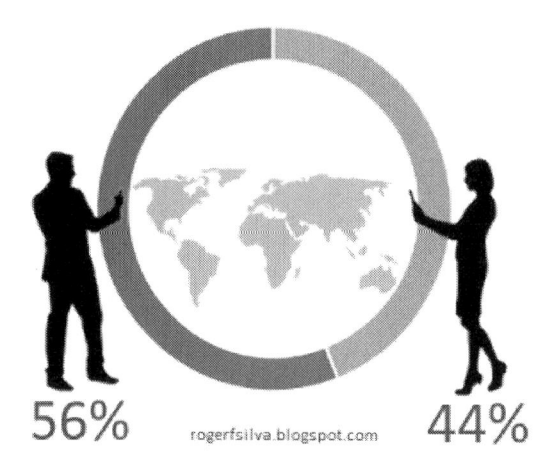

18- Insert a new text box and type "Smartphone Users". Move the text box as show in figure below.

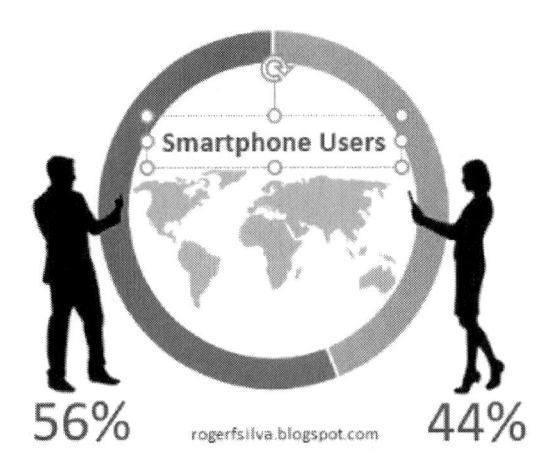

19- Congratulations! In few steps you have created a beautiful Infographic.

5. Exercise 3: Funnel Chart "Sales Pipeline".

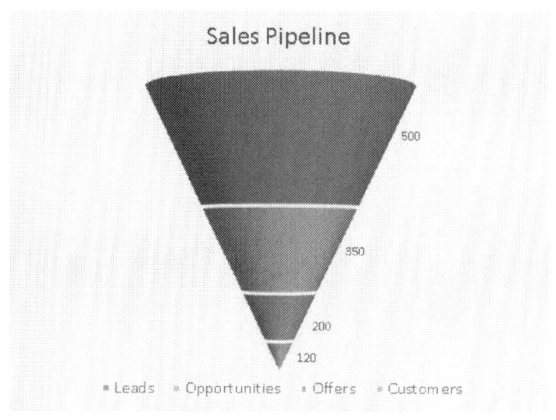

rogerfsilva.blogspot.com

Funnel Chart can be very useful to show stages and proportions in the sales process. Despite its importance, creating a nice Funnel Chart in Excel can be little tricky. In this step-by-step you will be able to create a nice one, following the example below.

1 - Type the data below.

Stage	Quantity
Leads	500
Opportunities	350
Offers	200
Customers	120

2 - With the cells selected Go to "Insert" tab, "Charts" group, 3-D Stacked Column.

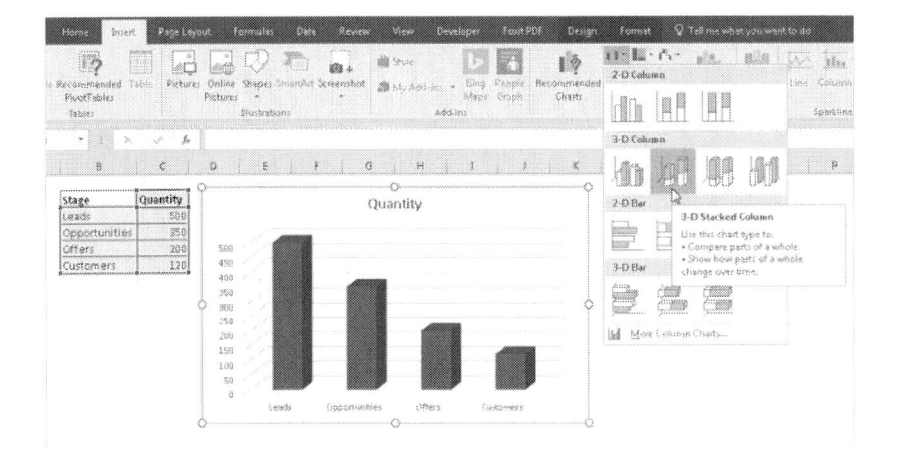

3 - With the chart selected, click in the option "Switch Row/Column".

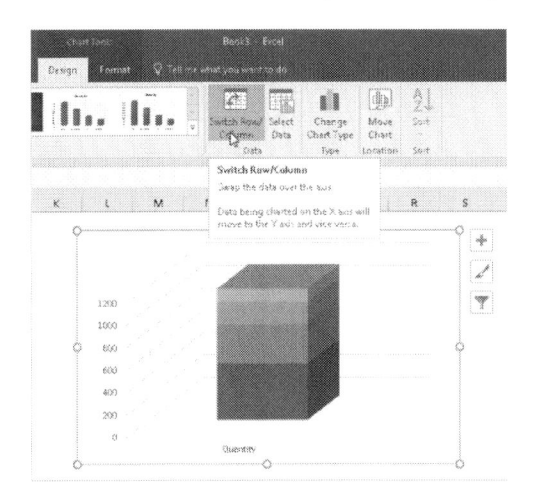

4 - Right click the Vertical axis on the chart and select "Format Chart Area", Select "Effects" and change the "X Rotation" and "Y Rotation" to "0" as the image below.

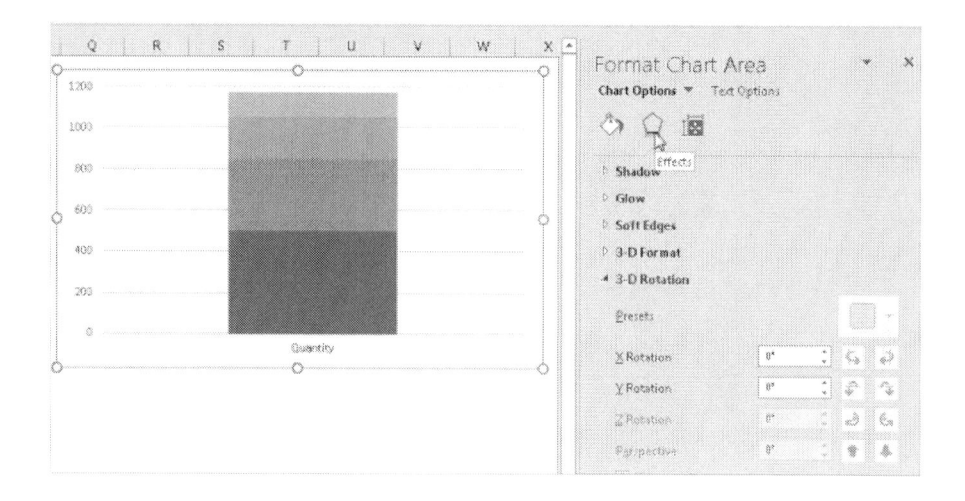

5 - Right Click any Series (bar items) and select "Format Data Series". Go to "Series Options" and set the "Gap Depth" to 150%, "Gap Width" to 80%, and select the "Full Cone" option.

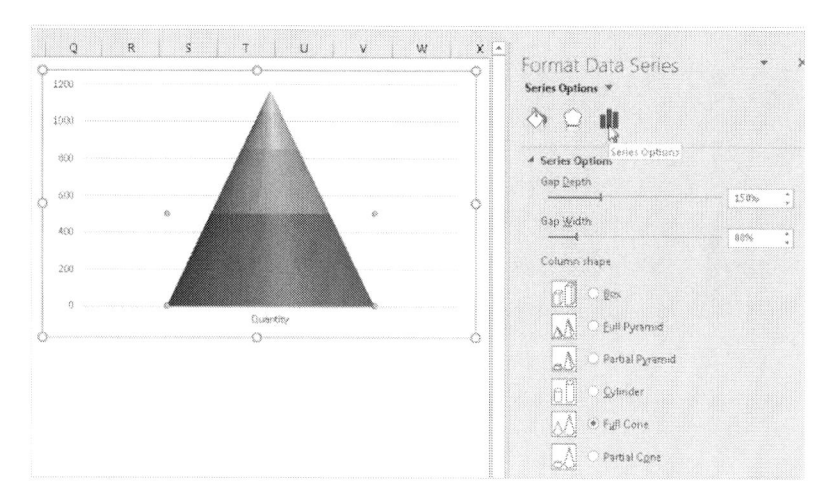

6 - Right click the "Vertical Axis" and select "Format Axis". Go to "Axis Options" and check the option "Values in reverse order".

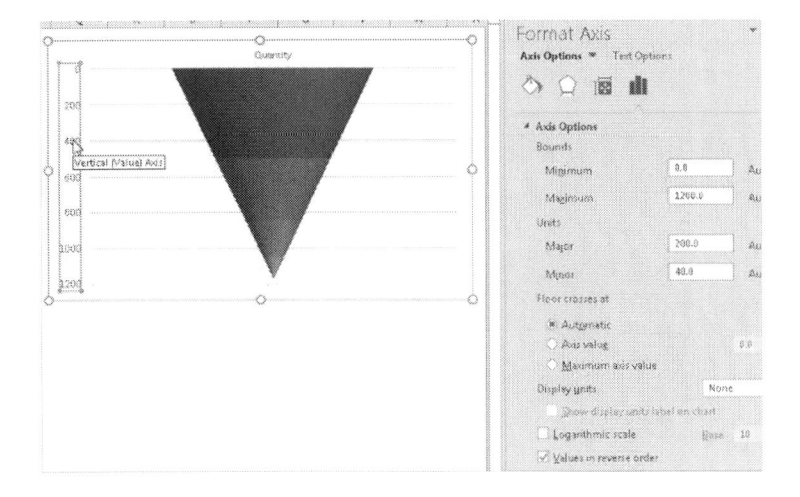

7 - Go to "Chart Elements" and let just the "Legend / Bottom" selected.

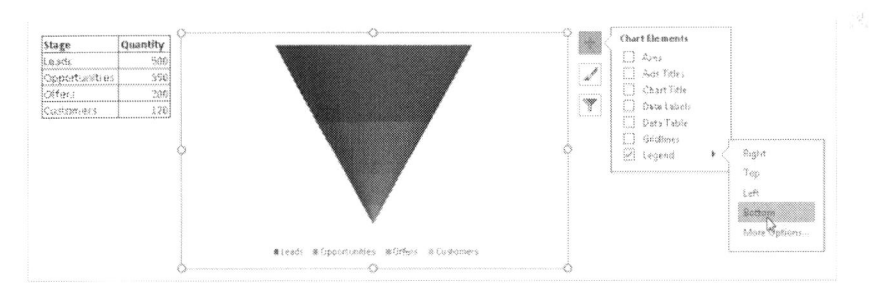

8 - Select the series and change the colors as your preferences.

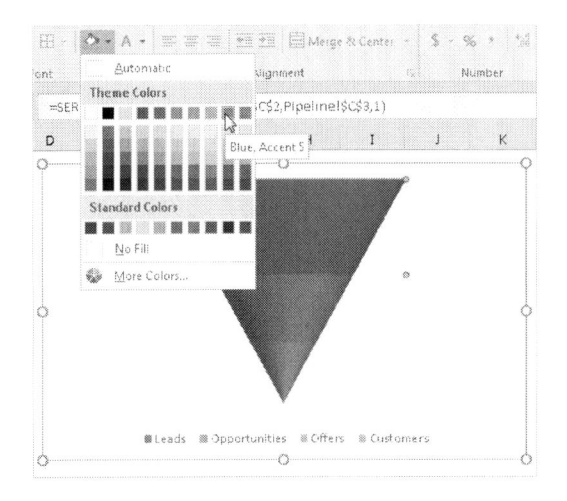

9 - Select each series and change the "Shape Outline" color to light grey and the weight to 3pt.

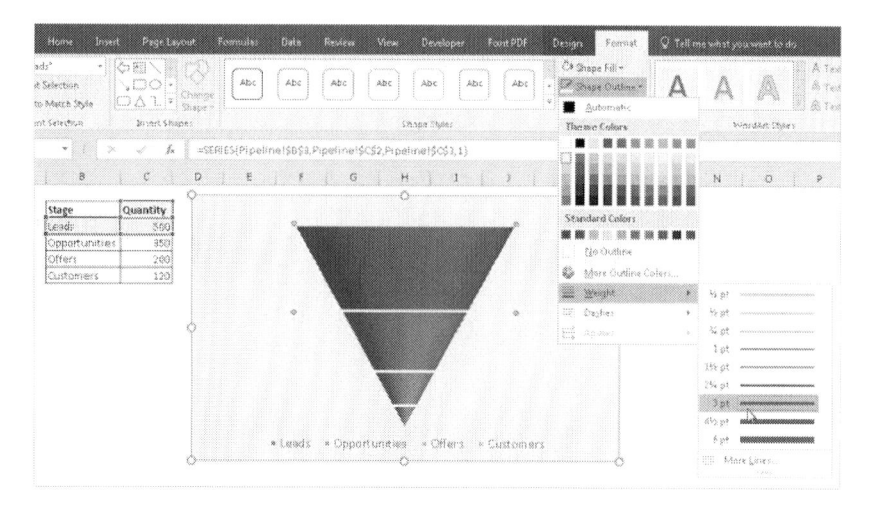

10 - If you want you can insert the "Chart Title" and "Data Labels" as the image below.

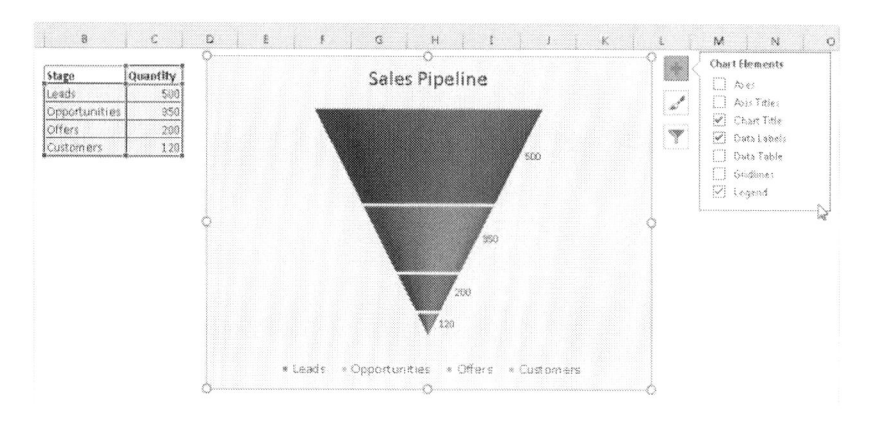

11 - To give it a "Round Edge" effect, go to "Format Chart Area", "Effects", "3-D Rotation" and set the "Perspective" as 15.

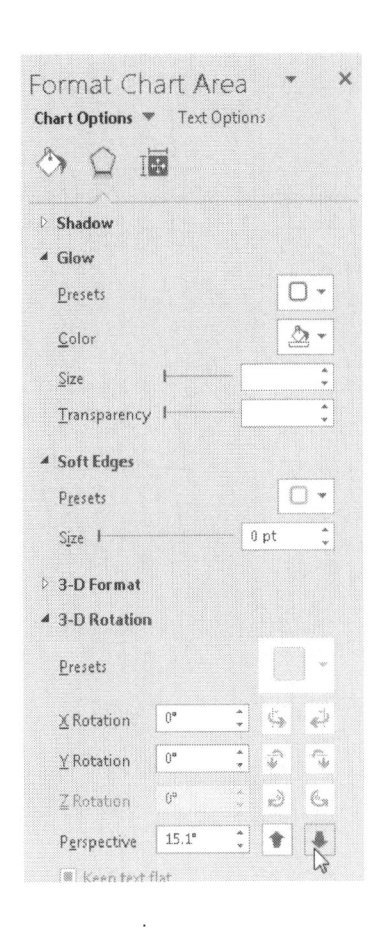

12 - Congratulations! You have created a Customized Funnel Chart! This is a useful, nice and professional look!

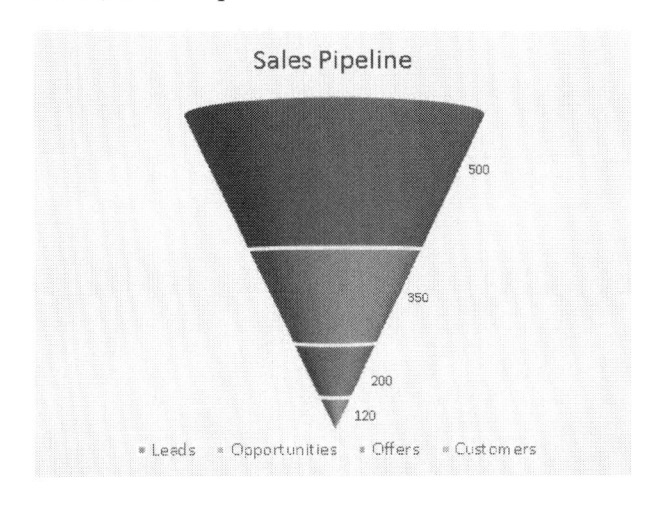

6. Exercise 4: Bar Chart "Customer Satisfaction"

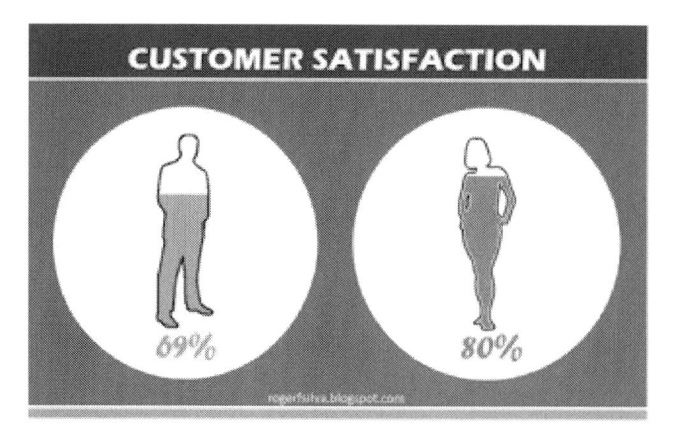

Studies have found that 90% of the information that we remember is based on visual impact. Try this step by step and learn how to use charts and pictures to create great eye-catching information.

1- Type the information words and numbers below in Range M3:N4.

	L	M	N
1			
2			
3		Men	100%
4		Women	100%

2- Type **CUSTOMER SATISFACTION** in cell A1.

	A	B	C
1	CUSTOMER SATISFACTION		
2			

3- Select Range A3:K20. Go to "Home" tab, "Font" group, "Fill Color" and select Grey 25%.

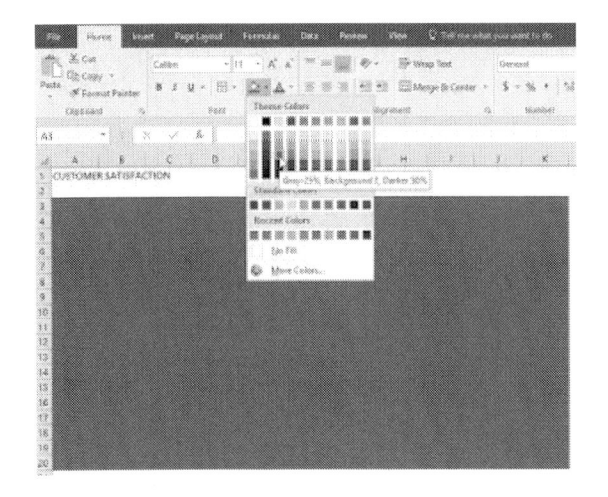

4- Go to "Insert" tab, "Illustrations" group, click on "Shapes" and select "Oval". Click and drag to create a circle.

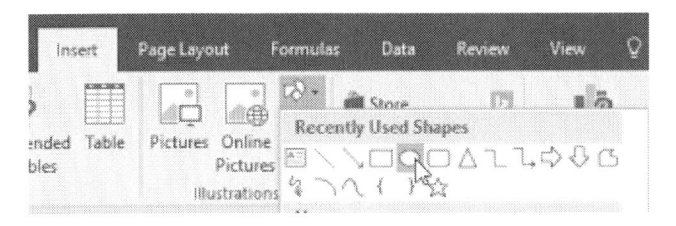

5- Go to "Format" tab, "Size" group and set the "Height" and "Width" to 8cm.

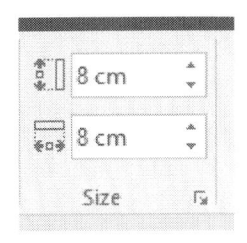

6- Go to "Format" tab, "Shape Outline" and select "No outline".

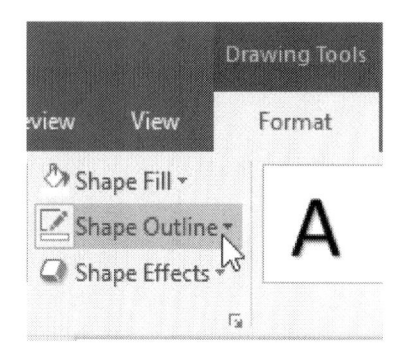

7- Copy and paste the shape and drag as figure below.

8- Select Range M3:N3. Go to "Insert" tab, "Charts" group, "Insert Column Bar" and select clustered column.

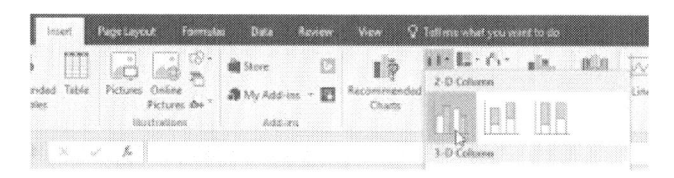

9- Right click the vertical Axis and select "Format Axis".

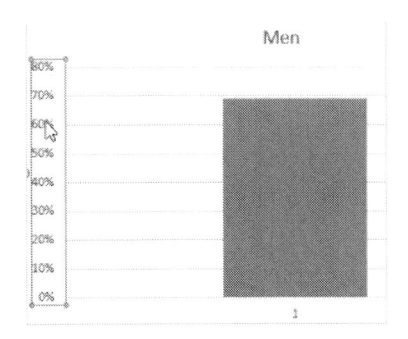

10- Go to "Axis Options", "Maximum" and type 1.0. "Minimum" and Type 0.0.

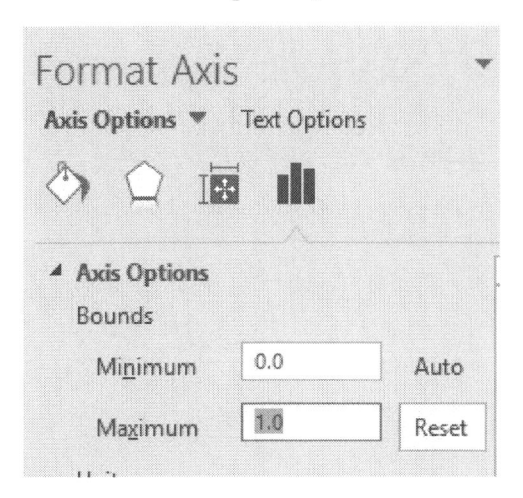

11- Delete the Axis, Titles, Legend and Gridlines.

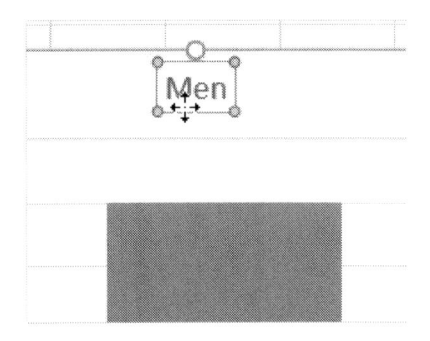

12- You can press "Delete" key or use the "Chart Elements" box.

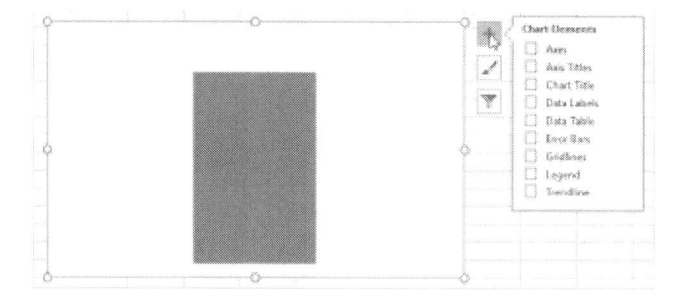

13- With the chart selected format "No Outline" and "No Fill",

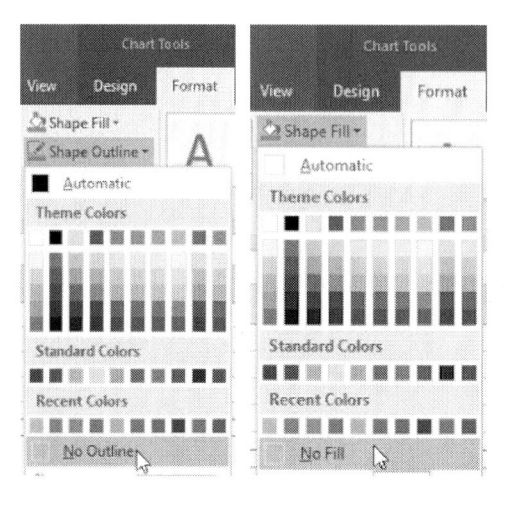

14- Go to "Page Layout'" tab, "Sheet Options" and deselect Gridlines View.

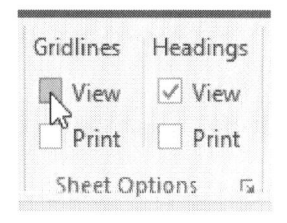

15- Double click the Series "Men", right click and select "Format Data Point".

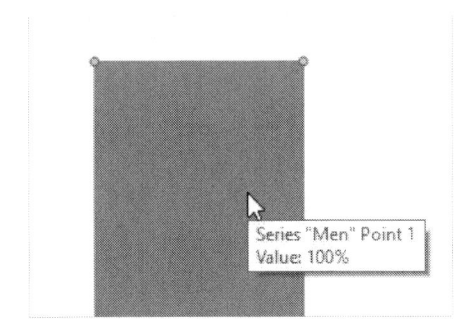

16- Go to "Series Options", "Gap Width" and type 0%.

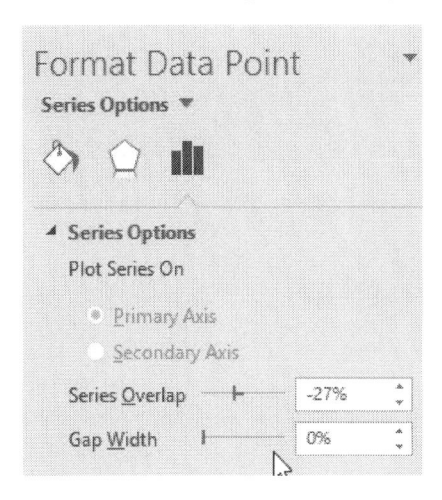

17- Go to "Format" tab, "Size" group and set "Height" 6.5cm and "Width" 2.5cm

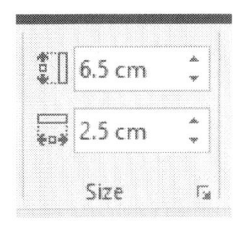

18- Go to "Shape Fill" and select "Gold, Accent 4" color.

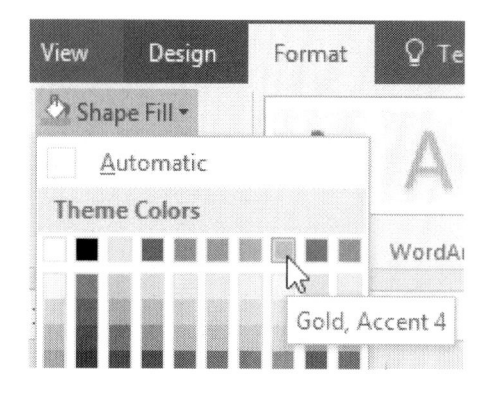

19- Copy the chart, select cell G4 and paste.

20- Click and drag the charts.

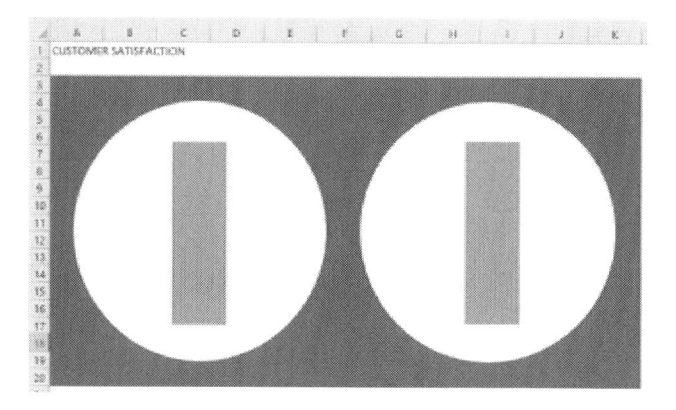

21- Select Right Chart, and change the data to Range M4:N4.

22- Double click the chart on Series "Woman". Go to "Shape Fill" and "More Fill Colors". Select as figure below.

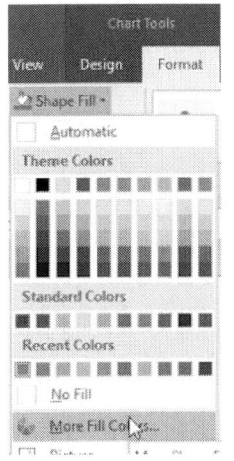

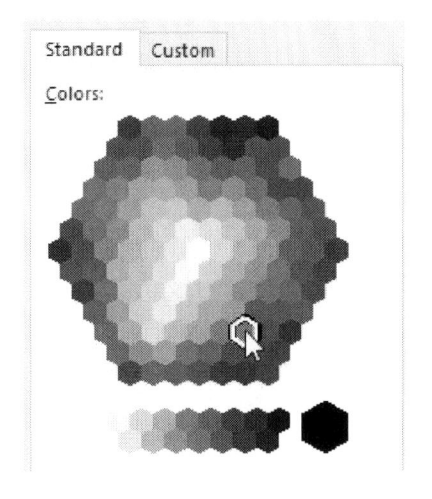

23- Your spreadsheet should be like this:

24- Remember that you can select the shapes or charts and Bring Forward or Send Backward by using the option below.

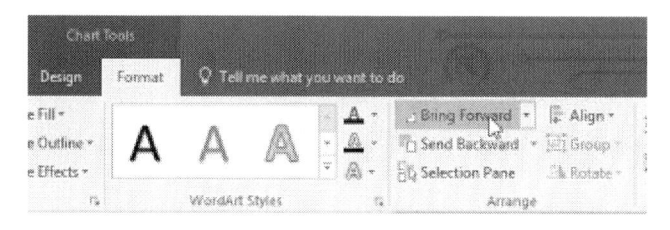

25- Go to the link below and save the image below (Man and Woman) by right clicking the image and selecting "Save image as".

http://rogerfsilva.blogspot.com/2017/06/book-dashboard.html

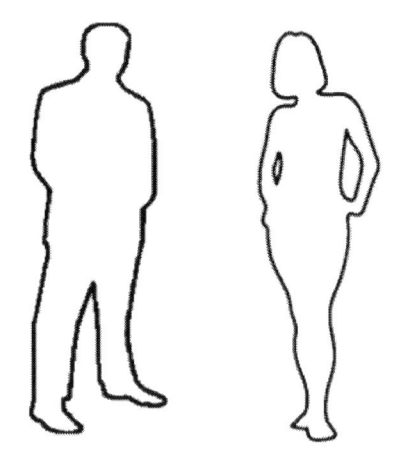

26- Go to "Insert" tab, "Illustrations" group, click in "Picture" and choose the images that you just saved.

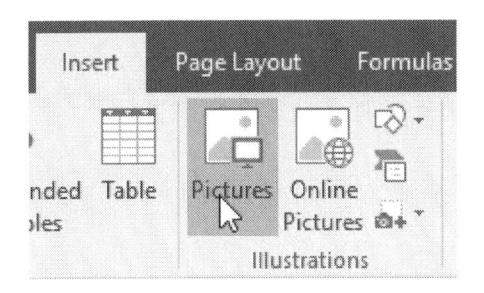

27- Change their Heights to 6.25cm.

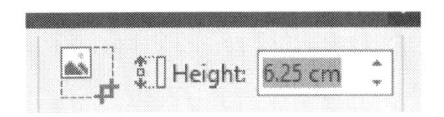

28- Click and drag the images over the charts. Change the values to 69% and 80%.

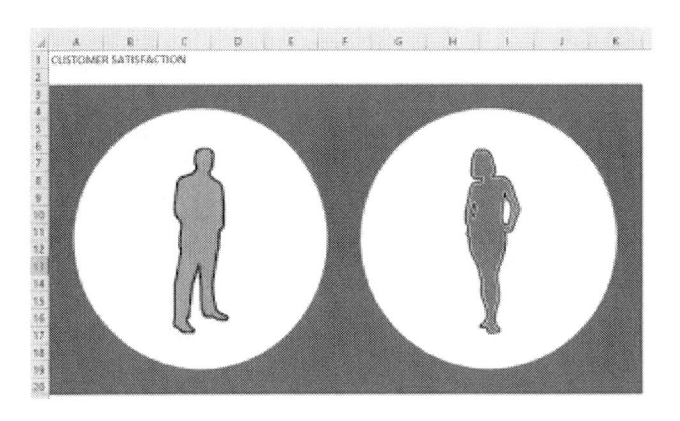

29- Go to "Insert" tab, "Text" group and click on "Text Box".

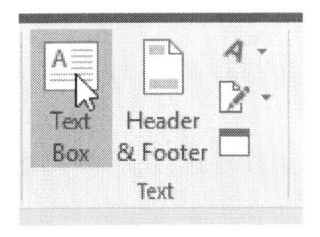

30- Click and drag to draw a Text Box. With the text box selected type in Formula Bar =N3 to link the N3 value into the text box.

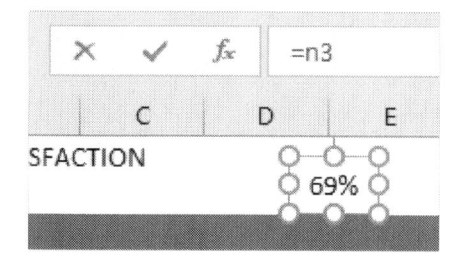

31- Create one more text box. Click and drag to draw a Text Box. With the text box selected type in Formula Bar =N4 to link the N4 value into the text box.

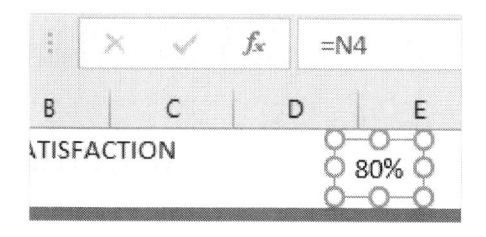

32- Configure each text box as image below. "Forte Font", "Size 28", and colors. Click and drag them.

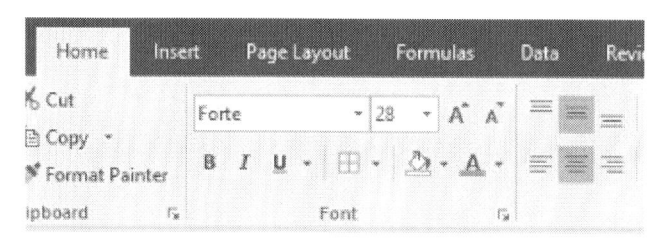

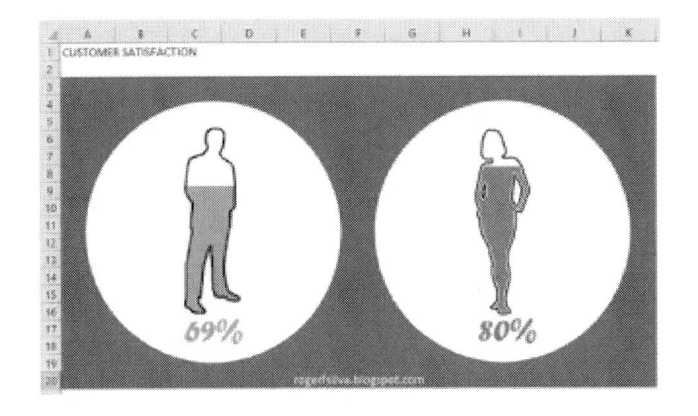

33-Select Range A1:K1. Go to "Home" tab, "Alignment" group and select "Merge & Center".

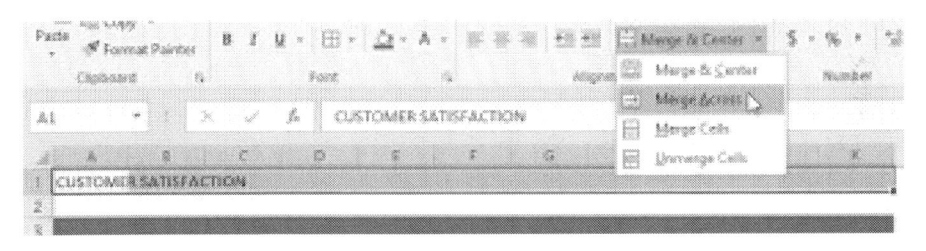

34- Configure the Range as image below. "Eras Bold Font", "Size 26", "Font Color White", " Fill Color, Grey -25%, Darker 75%", "Bottom Align" and "Center".

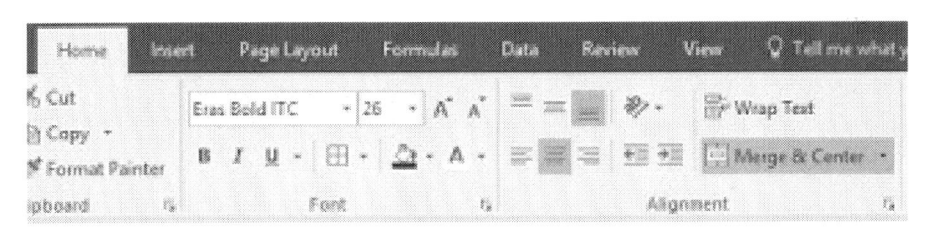

35- Change Row1 height to 45.

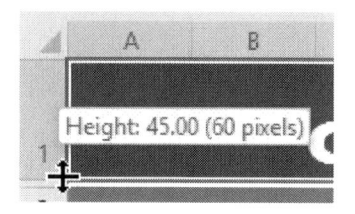

36- Change Row2 height to 3.

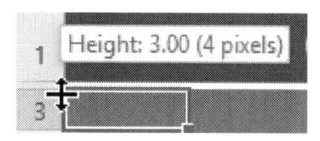

37- Change Row 21 height to 3.

38- Select Range A22:K22 and change color.

39- Change Row 22 height to 7.50.

40- Congratulations! You have used Chart and Pictures to create an Eye-Catching .... Information.

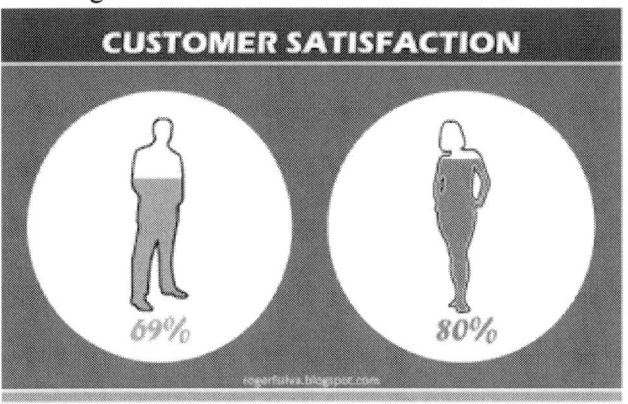

7. Sales Dashboard

The most valuable commodity I know of is information.
- Gordon Gekko, Wall Street movie.

Before starting the Sales Dashboard construction, be sure that you have reviewed the exercises available in this book, they are important to help you understanding the basics of tables and chart creation and customization.

The Dashboard that you will be creating is a Sales Dashboard, that will show the key performance indicators from sales and marketing area and, the sales history details.

Through the Timeline and slicer, you will be able to filter your data and give you more insights.

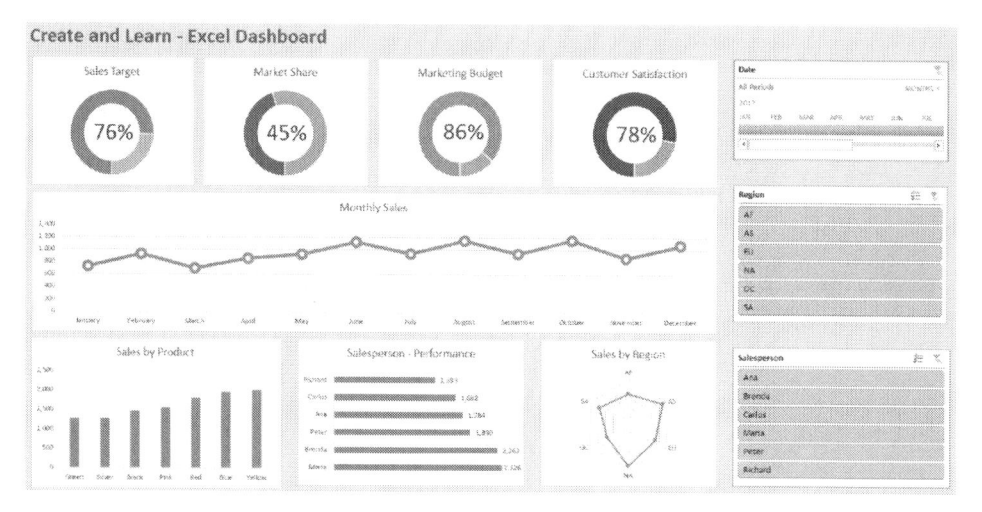

1. Data Formatting

1- First, we will need to have the data that will be used in the Dashboard. Go to http://rogerfsilva.blogspot.com/2017/06/books.html
Find the table "Dashboard book" select the table and copy.

Date	Product	Client	Salesperson	Region	US$
1/01/2017	Blue	Viper	Peter	SA	180
1/02/2017	Yellow	MicroT	Maria	NA	210
1/03/2017	Red	Tanka	Richard	OC	80
1/04/2017	Green	Bravo	Carlos	AF	75
1/05/2017	Black	TBK	Ana	EU	150
1/06/2017	Pink	Viper	Brenda	AS	250
1/07/2017	Silver	MicroT	Peter	SA	180
1/08/2017	Blue	Tanka	Maria	NA	210
1/09/2017	Yellow	Bravo	Richard	OC	240
1/10/2017	Red	TBK	Carlos	AF	270
1/11/2017	Green	Viper	Ana	EU	300
1/12/2017	Black	MicroT	Brenda	AS	330
1/01/2017	Pink	Tanka	Peter	SA	165
1/02/2017	Silver	Bravo	Maria	NA	275
1/03/2017	Blue	TBK	Richard	OC	198
1/04/2017	Yellow	Viper	Carlos	AF	231
1/05/2017	Red	MicroT	Ana	EU	264
1/06/2017	Green	Tanka	Brenda	AS	297
1/07/2017	Black	Bravo	Peter	SA	330
1/08/2017	Pink	TBK	Maria	NA	363
1/09/2017	Silver	Viper	Richard	OC	181.5
1/10/2017	Blue	MicroT	Carlos	AF	302.5
1/11/2017	Yellow	Tanka	Ana	EU	217.8
1/12/2017	Red	Bravo	Brenda	AS	254.1
1/01/2017	Blue	Viper	Peter	SA	180
1/02/2017	Yellow	MicroT	Maria	NA	210
1/03/2017	Red	Tanka	Richard	OC	80

(Ask Cortana / Select all / Copy)

*Below you can also find the full data set.

Month	Product	Client	Seller	Region	US$
1/01/2017	Blue	Viper	Peter	SA	180.00
1/02/2017	Yellow	MicroT	Maria	NA	210.00
1/03/2017	Red	Tanka	Richard	OC	80.00
1/04/2017	Green	Bravo	Carlos	AF	75.00
1/05/2017	Black	TBK	Ana	EU	150.00
1/06/2017	Pink	Viper	Brenda	AS	250.00
1/07/2017	Silver	MicroT	Peter	SA	180.00
1/08/2017	Blue	Tanka	Maria	NA	210.00
1/09/2017	Yellow	Bravo	Richard	OC	240.00
1/10/2017	Red	TBK	Carlos	AF	270.00
1/11/2017	Green	Viper	Ana	EU	300.00
1/12/2017	Black	MicroT	Brenda	AS	330.00
1/01/2017	Pink	Tanka	Peter	SA	165.00
1/02/2017	Silver	Bravo	Maria	NA	275.00
1/03/2017	Blue	TBK	Richard	OC	198.00
1/04/2017	Yellow	Viper	Carlos	AF	231.00
1/05/2017	Red	MicroT	Ana	EU	264.00
1/06/2017	Green	Tanka	Brenda	AS	297.00
1/07/2017	Black	Bravo	Peter	SA	330.00
1/08/2017	Pink	TBK	Maria	NA	363.00
1/09/2017	Silver	Viper	Richard	OC	181.50
1/10/2017	Blue	MicroT	Carlos	AF	302.50
1/11/2017	Yellow	Tanka	Ana	EU	217.80
1/12/2017	Red	Bravo	Brenda	AS	254.10
1/01/2017	Blue	Viper	Peter	SA	180.00
1/02/2017	Yellow	MicroT	Maria	NA	210.00
1/03/2017	Red	Tanka	Richard	OC	80.00
1/04/2017	Pink	Viper	Brenda	AS	250.00
1/05/2017	Silver	MicroT	Peter	SA	180.00
1/06/2017	Blue	Tanka	Maria	NA	210.00
1/07/2017	Yellow	Bravo	Richard	OC	240.00
1/08/2017	Red	TBK	Carlos	AF	270.00
1/09/2017	Green	Viper	Ana	EU	300.00
1/10/2017	Black	MicroT	Brenda	AS	330.00

1/11/2017	Pink	Tanka	Peter	SA		165.00
1/12/2017	Silver	Bravo	Maria	NA		275.00
1/01/2017	Blue	TBK	Richard	OC		198.00
1/02/2017	Yellow	Viper	Carlos	AF		231.00
1/03/2017	Red	MicroT	Ana	EU		264.00
1/04/2017	Green	Tanka	Brenda	AS		297.00
1/05/2017	Black	Bravo	Peter	SA		330.00
1/06/2017	Pink	TBK	Maria	NA		363.00
1/07/2017	Silver	Viper	Richard	OC		181.50
1/08/2017	Blue	MicroT	Carlos	AF		302.50
1/09/2017	Yellow	Tanka	Ana	EU		217.80
1/10/2017	Red	Bravo	Brenda	AS		254.10
1/11/2017	Blue	Viper	Peter	SA		180.00
1/12/2017	Yellow	MicroT	Maria	NA		210.00

2- Create a new excel file and rename "Sheet1" to "Data".

3- Select cell A1 and go to press "Crt+V" or click on "Paste".

	A	B	C	D	E	F
1	Date	Product	Client	Salesperson	Region	US$
2	1/01/2017	Blue	Viper	Peter	SA	180
3	1/02/2017	Yellow	MicroT	Maria	NA	210
4	1/03/2017	Red	Tanka	Richard	OC	80
5	1/04/2017	Green	Bravo	Carlos	AF	75
6	1/05/2017	Black	TBK	Ana	EU	150
7	1/06/2017	Pink	Viper	Brenda	AS	250
8	1/07/2017	Silver	MicroT	Peter	SA	180
9	1/08/2017	Blue	Tanka	Maria	NA	210
10	1/09/2017	Yellow	Bravo	Richard	OC	240
11	1/10/2017	Red	TBK	Carlos	AF	270
12	1/11/2017	Green	Viper	Ana	EU	300
13	1/12/2017	Black	MicroT	Brenda	AS	330
14	1/01/2017	Pink	Tanka	Peter	SA	165
15	1/02/2017	Silver	Bravo	Maria	NA	275
16	1/03/2017	Blue	TBK	Richard	OC	198

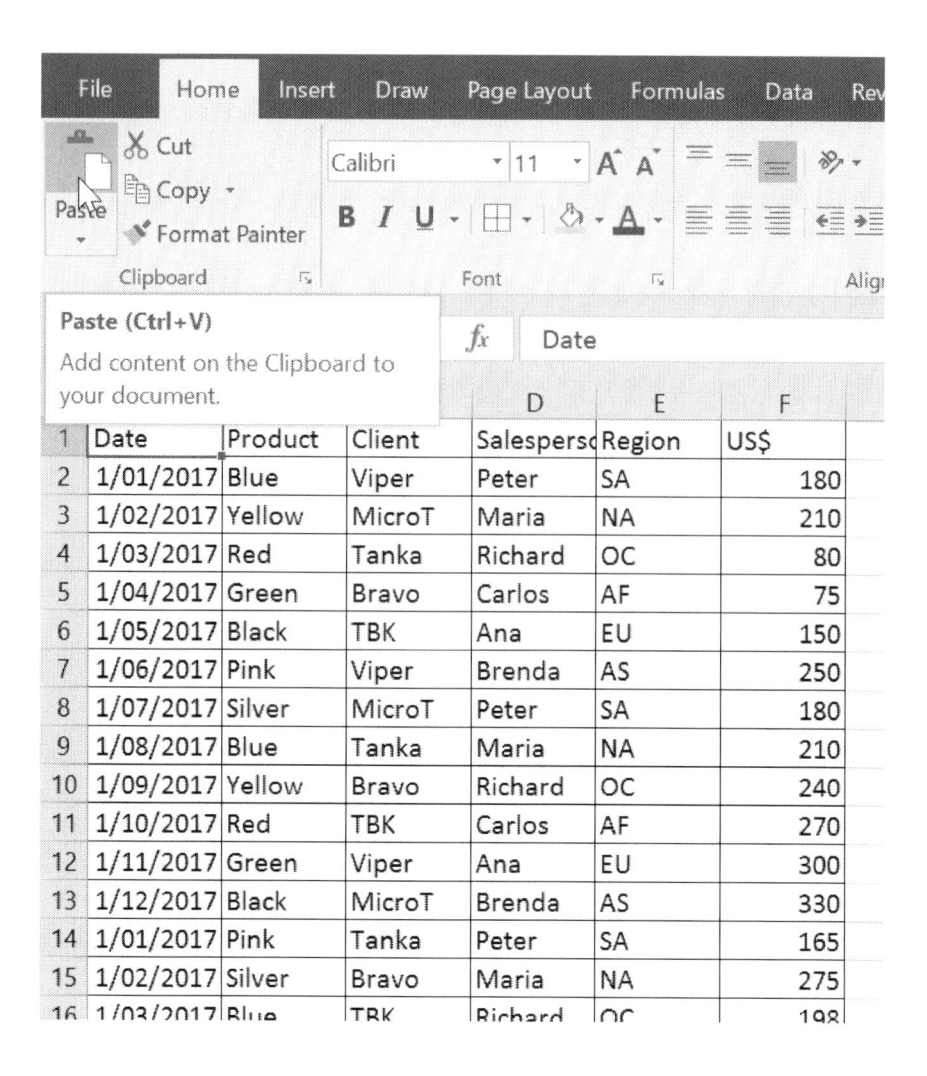

4- Go to "Page Layout'" tab, "Sheet Options" and deselect Gridlines View.

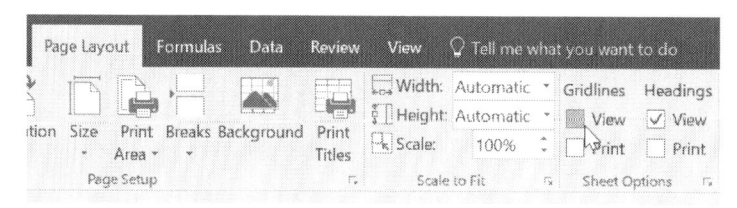

5- Select Range A1:F50.

	A	B	C	D	E	F
1	Date	Product	Client	Salesperso	Region	US$
2	1/01/2017	Blue	Viper	Peter	SA	180
3	1/02/2017	Yellow	MicroT	Maria	NA	210
4	1/03/2017	Red	Tanka	Richard	OC	80
5	1/04/2017	Green	Bravo	Carlos	AF	75
6	1/05/2017	Black	TBK	Ana	EU	150
7	1/06/2017	Pink	Viper	Brenda	AS	250
8	1/07/2017	Silver	MicroT	Peter	SA	180
9	1/08/2017	Blue	Tanka	Maria	NA	210
10	1/09/2017	Yellow	Bravo	Richard	OC	240
11	1/10/2017	Red	TBK	Carlos	AF	270
12	1/11/2017	Green	Viper	Ana	EU	300
13	1/12/2017	Black	MicroT	Brenda	AS	330

6- Go to "Home" tab, "Format as Table" and select the theme "Blue".

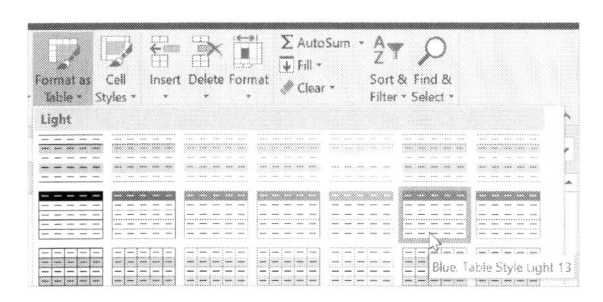

7- The "Format as Table" message will appear, check if the range is correct, check the option "My table has headers" and click "OK".

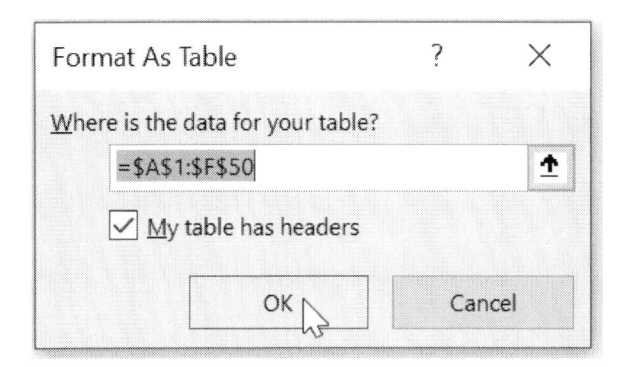

8- Your range will be formatted as table, and should look like the image below.

	A	B	C	D	E	F
1	Date	Product	Client	Salesperson	Region	US$
2	1/01/2017	Blue	Viper	Peter	SA	180
3	1/02/2017	Yellow	MicroT	Maria	NA	210
4	1/03/2017	Red	Tanka	Richard	OC	80
5	1/04/2017	Green	Bravo	Carlos	AF	75
6	1/05/2017	Black	TBK	Ana	EU	150

9- Go to column I and insert the values according to the image below.

	F	G	H	I	J	K
1	US$		Sales Target			
2	180		Target	15000		
3	210		Sales		Addition	
4	80		Gap		Subtraction	
5	75		%		Division	
6	150		Double Check		Multiplication	
7	250					
8	180		Market Share			
9	210		Market	1		
10	240		Company Market Share	0.45		
11	270		Gap		Subtraction	
12	300					
13	330		Marketing Budget			
14	165		Plan	500		
15	275		Actual	430		
16	198		Balance		Subtraction	
17	231		%		Division	
18	264					
19	297		Customer Satisfaction			
20	330		Survey	1		
21	363		Customer Satisfaction	0.78		
22	181.5		Gap		Subtraction	

10- Move your mouse between columns J and K, when your pointer change the format below, double click or click+hold+drag to change the column width.

11- Select range "H2 to J6".

12- Go to the "Home Tab", "Font group", click on "Border" and select "All borders".

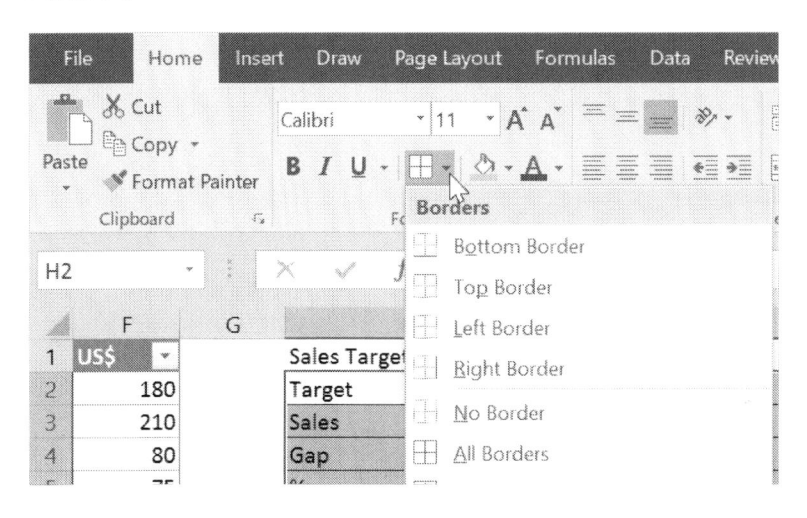

13- Go to cell I2 and change the select color "Gold", to identify this cell as an input cell.

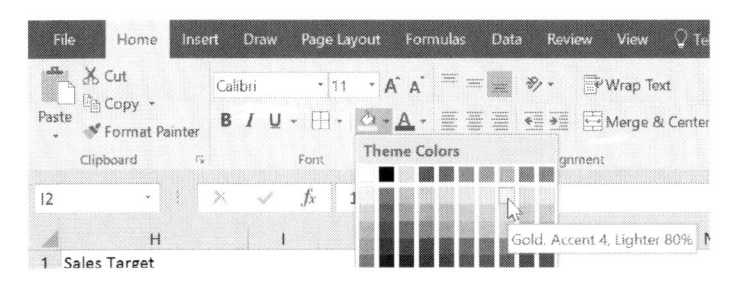

14- Select range I2 to I6 and color "Light Grey" to identify that these cells contain formula.

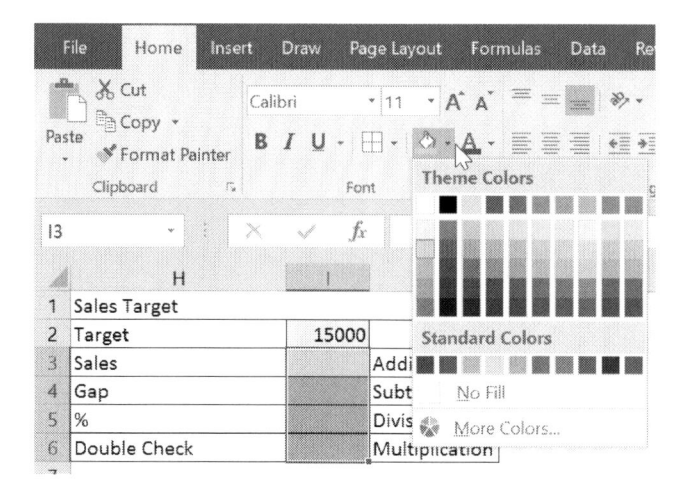

15- Repeat the steps to have the same result as image below.

16- Select cell A2, go to "Design tab", "Resize table group", and change the Table Name to "tbData".

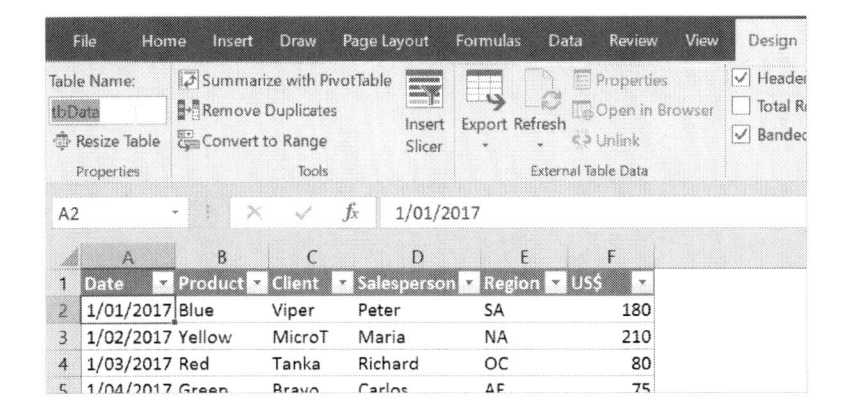

2. Working with formulas

17- Go to cell I3 and type the sum formula **=sum(F2:F50)** and press Enter. This formula will sum the range F2 to F50 ($ sales amount).

	H	I
1	Sales Target	
2	Target	15000
3	Sales	=sum(F2:F50)

18- Go to cell I4 and type the subtraction formula **=I2-I3** and press Enter. This formula will give you the difference between sales target and current sales.

SUM   × ✓ *fx*   =I2-I3

	H	I	J
1	Sales Target		
2	Target	15000	
3	Sales	11342.8	Addition
4	Gap	=I2-I3	Subtraction

19- Go to I5 and type the division formula **=I3/I2**. This formula will help to find the percentage of accomplishment.

SUM   × ✓ *fx*   =I3/I2

	H	I	J
1	Sales Target		
2	Target	15000	
3	Sales	11342.8	Addition
4	Gap	3657.2	Subtraction
5	%	=I3/I2	Division
6	Double Check		Multiplication

20- Go to cell I6 and type the multiplication formula =I5*I2. This formula will double check your formulas and will return the sales amount.

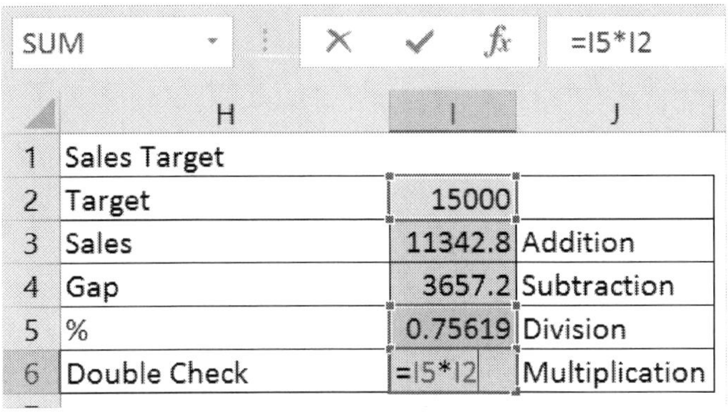

	H	I	J
1	Sales Target		
2	Target	15000	
3	Sales	11342.8	Addition
4	Gap	3657.2	Subtraction
5	%	0.75619	Division
6	Double Check	=I5*I2	Multiplication

21- Select range I3 to I4. Go to "Home tab", "Number group" and select comma style.

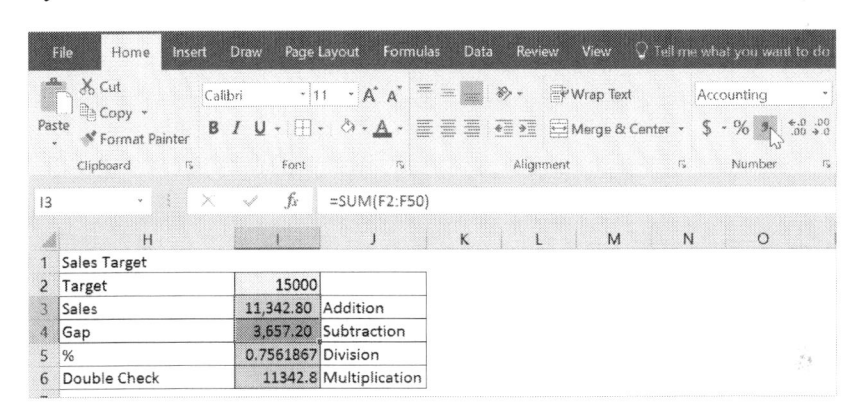

	H	I	J
1	Sales Target		
2	Target	15000	
3	Sales	11,342.80	Addition
4	Gap	3,657.20	Subtraction
5	%	0.7561867	Division
6	Double Check	11342.8	Multiplication

22- Go to decrease decimals and click till the decimals places are gone.

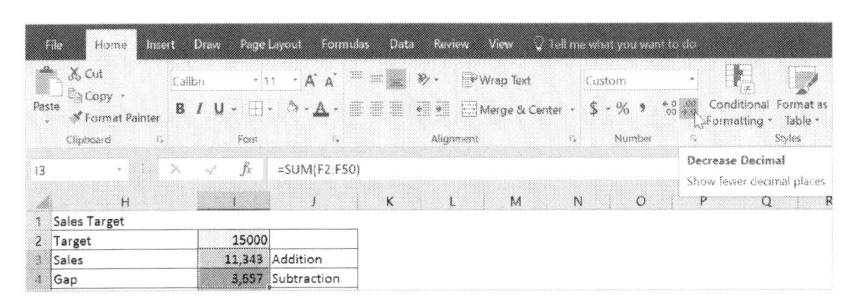

	H	I	J
1	Sales Target		
2	Target	15000	
3	Sales	11,343	Addition
4	Gap	3,657	Subtraction

23- Select I5 and click on "Percent Style".

H	I	J
1 Sales Target		
2 Target	15000	
3 Sales	11,343	Addition
4 Gap	3,657	Subtraction
5 %	76%	Division

24- Now, go to I11 and type the formula =I9-I10.

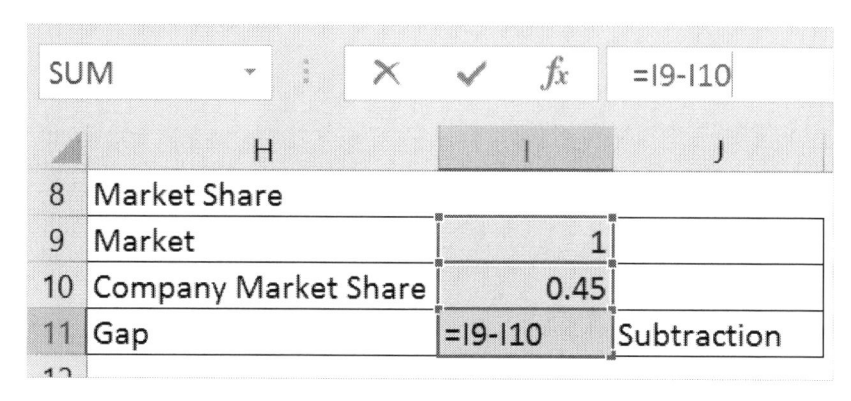

	H	I	J
8	Market Share		
9	Market	1	
10	Company Market Share	0.45	
11	Gap	=I9-I10	Subtraction

25- Go to I16 and type the formula =I14-I15.

	H	I	J
13	Marketing Budget		
14	Plan	500	
15	Actual	430	
16	Balance	=I14-I15	Subtraction
17	%		Division

26- Go to I17 and type the formula =I15/I14.

SUM		× ✓ f_x	=I15/I14	
	H		I	J
13	Marketing Budget			
14	Plan		500	
15	Actual		430	
16	Balance		70	Subtraction
17	%		=I15/I14	Division

27- Go to I22 and type the formula =I20-I21.

SUM		× ✓ f_x	=I20-I21	
	H		I	J
19	Customer Satisfaction			
20	Survey		1	
21	Customer Satisfaction		0.78	
22	Gap		=I20-I21	Subtraction

28- Format the cells to looks like the image below.

	F	G	H	I	J
1	US$		Sales Target		
2	180		Target	15,000.00	
3	210		Sales	11,342.80	Addition
4	80		Gap	3,657.20	Subtraction
5	75		%	76%	Division
6	150		Double Check	11,343	Multiplication
7	250				
8	180		Market Share		
9	210		Market	100%	
10	240		Company Market Share	45%	
11	270		Gap	55%	Subtraction
12	300				
13	330		Marketing Budget		
14	165		Plan	500	
15	275		Actual	430	
16	198		Balance	70	Subtraction
17	231		%	86%	Division
18	264				
19	297		Customer Satisfaction		
20	330		Survey	100%	
21	363		Customer Satisfaction	78%	
22	182		Gap	22%	Subtraction
23	303				

3. Creating PivotTables

29- Go close to the tab name and add a new sheet by clicking on "New Sheet".

30- Double click the new tab created and type a new name "Dashboard". You can also right click the tab and click on "Rename".

31- Click+Hold+Drag to move the Dashboard tab to the beginning.

32- Create new tabs and rename them to have eight tabs with the names: Dashboard, Training, Data, Moth, Product, Salesperson, Region, and Draft.

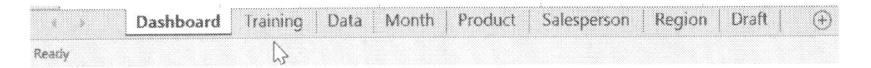

33- To create new tabs, you can also right click an existing tab and select "Insert".

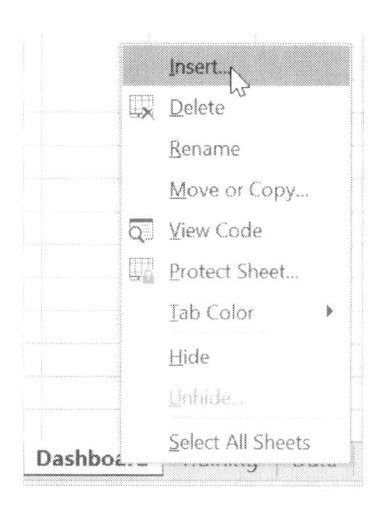

34- Uncheck the gridlines to each new tab.

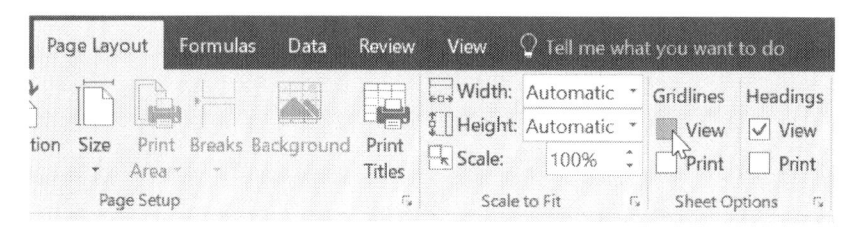

35- Select the tab "Month"

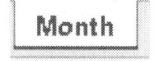

36- Select cell A3. Go to "Insert tab" and click on PivotTable.

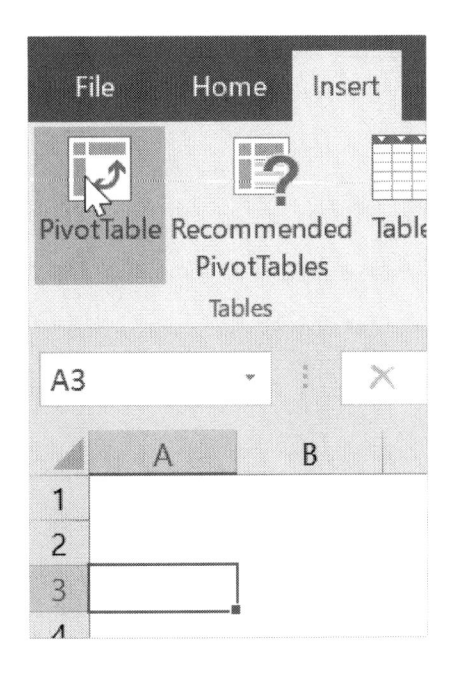

37- On the window "Create PivotTable", set the range as "tbData", and Location "Month!$A$3". Click Ok.

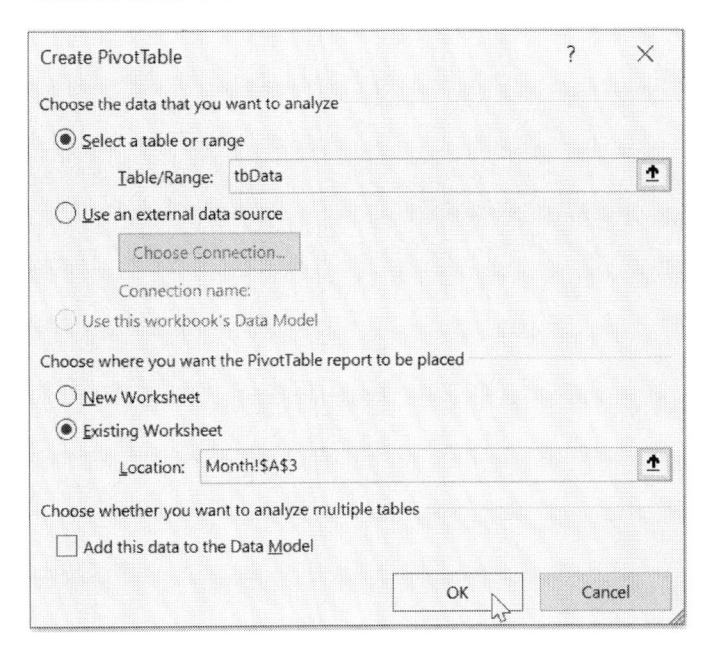

38- Select cell A3 and go to "Analyze tab", "PivotTable group", and change the PivotTable Name to "pvtMonth".

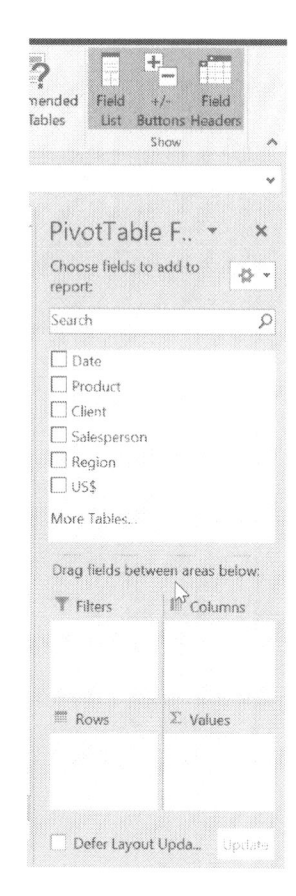

39- Go to "Analyze tab", "Show group", and be sure that the "Field List" is enable.

40- Click and drag the field "Date" to "Rows" section, and "US$" to "Values" section.

Note: If you drag any other field by mistake, just click on it and select "Remove Field"

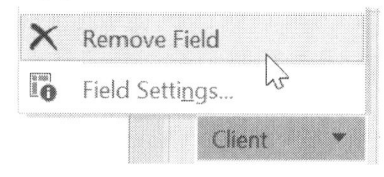

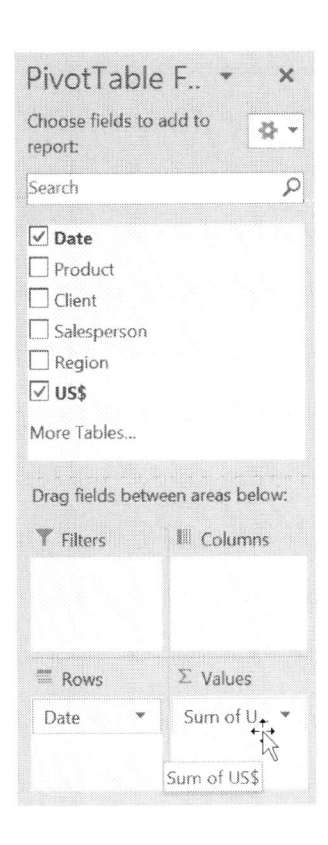

41- Go to Values section, and click on "Sum of US$", it will show an option list, select "Value field settings".

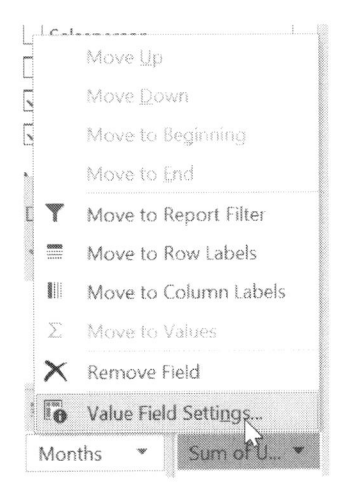

42- Set the calculation field as "Sum" and click on "Number Format".

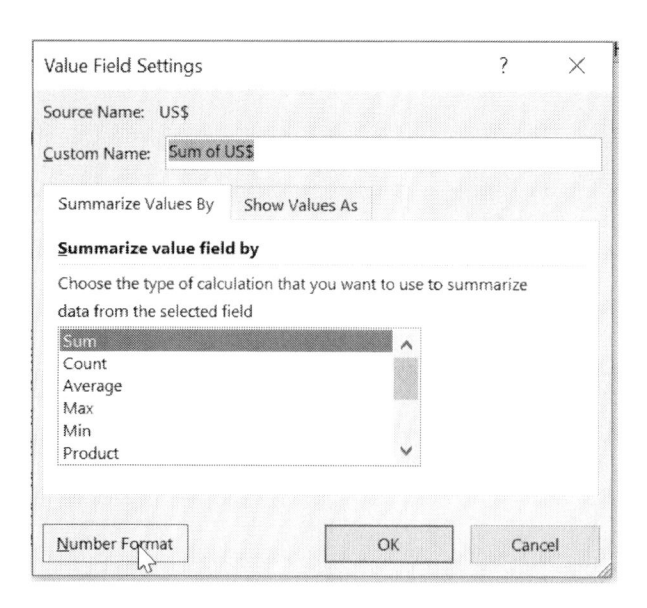

43- Select category "Number", set decimal places as zero and check "Use 1000 separator".

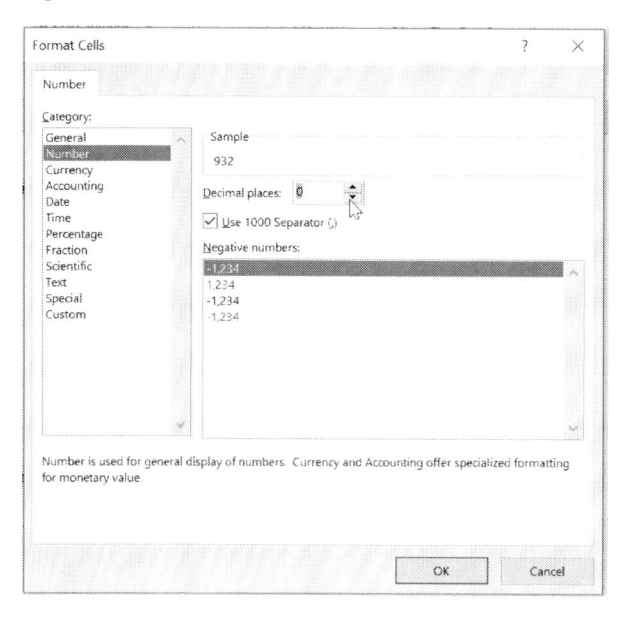

44- Right click A4 (where you have months) and click on "Ungroup".

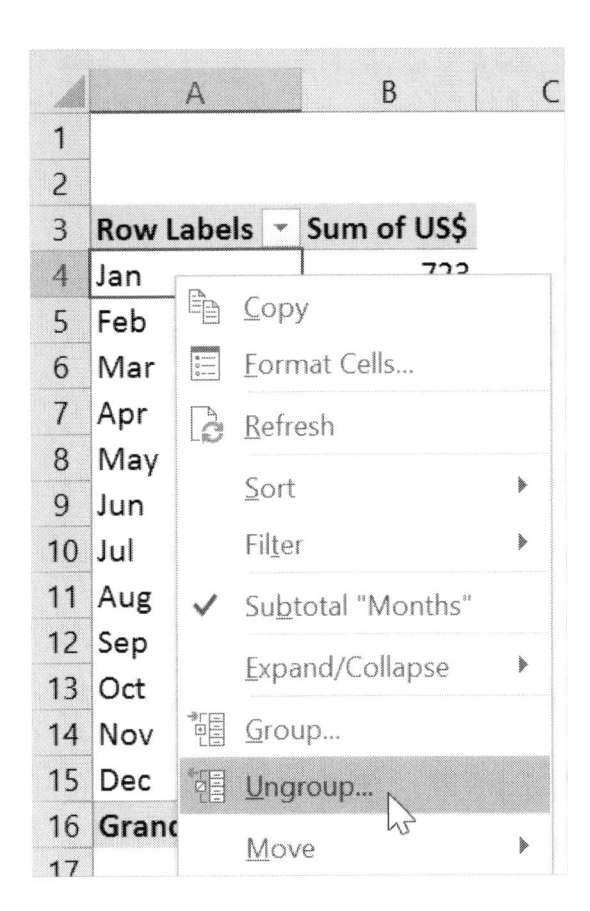

45- On the "Field List" click on "Date", "Field Settings" and then "Number Format".

46- Select "Custom". Type "mmmm", it will show a complete month name.

47- With A3 still selected go to "Design tab", "PivotTable Styles group" and change the style to "Light Blue".

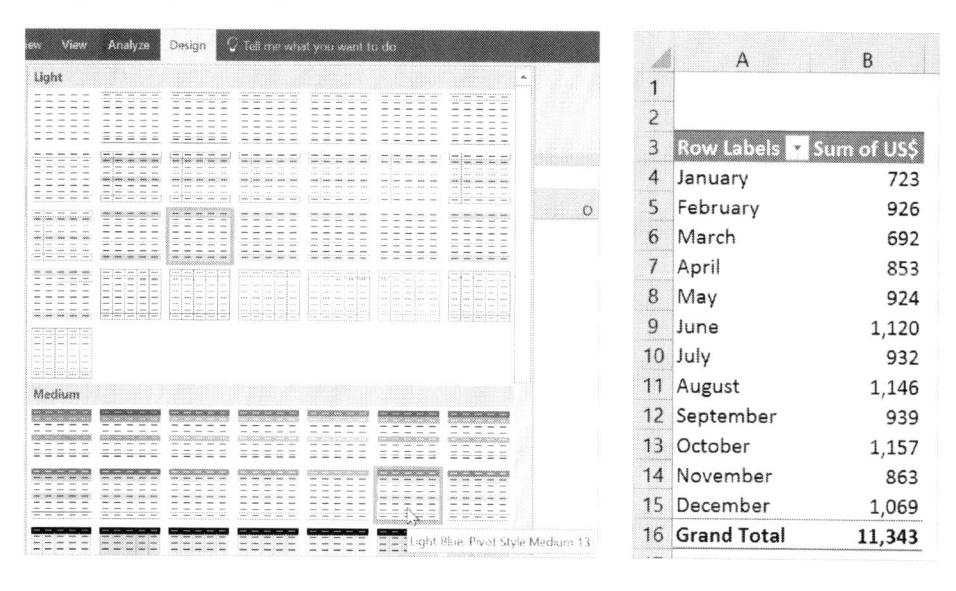

48- Select the PivotTable and copy.

	A	B
3	Row Labels	Sum of US$
4	January	723
5	February	926
6	March	692
7	April	853
8	May	924
9	June	1,120
10	July	932
11	August	1,146
12	September	939
13	October	1,157
14	November	863
15	December	1,069
16	Grand Total	11,343

49- Go to "Product", "A3" and paste the PivotTable. Change the "PivotTable Name" to "pvtProduct".

Row Labels	Sum of US$
January	723
February	926
March	692
April	853
May	924
June	1,120
July	932
August	1,146
September	939
October	1,157
November	863
December	1,069
Grand Total	**11,343**

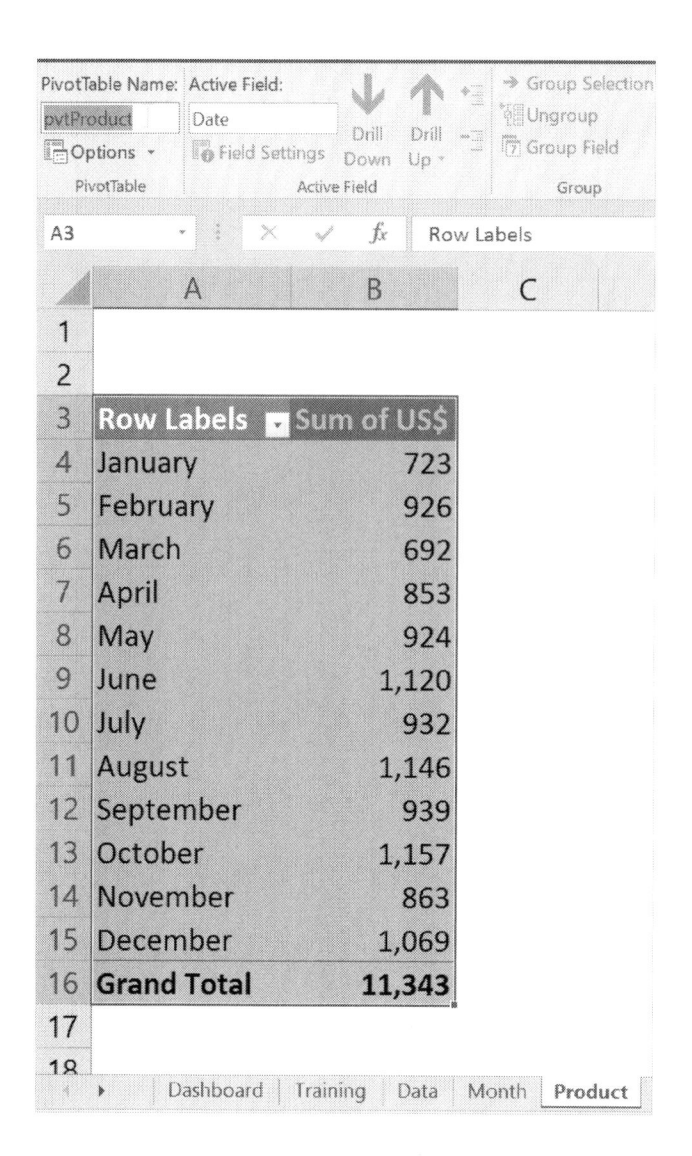

50- Paste the same PivotTable in the sheets "Sales Person" and "Region", change the names to "pvtSalesperson" and "pvtRegion".

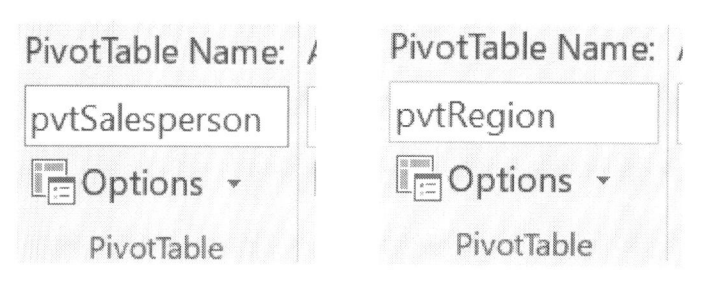

4. Creating PivotCharts

51- Go to "Month" tab and click on A3.

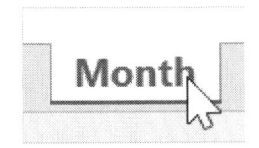

52- Go to "Analyze tab", "Tools group" and "PivotChart".

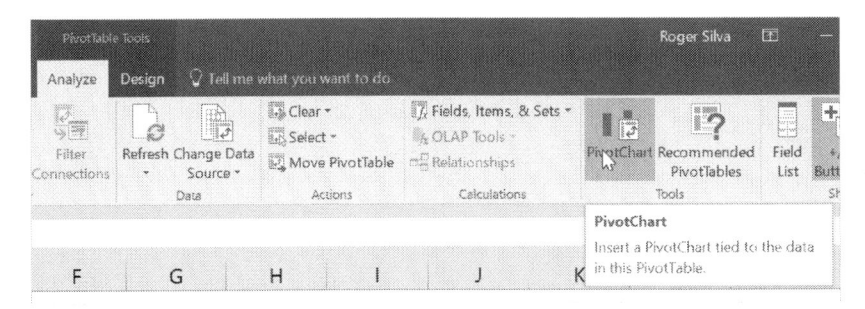

53- Select "Line" chart and click "OK".

54- Select the new chart and go to "Analyze tab" and click on "Move Chart".

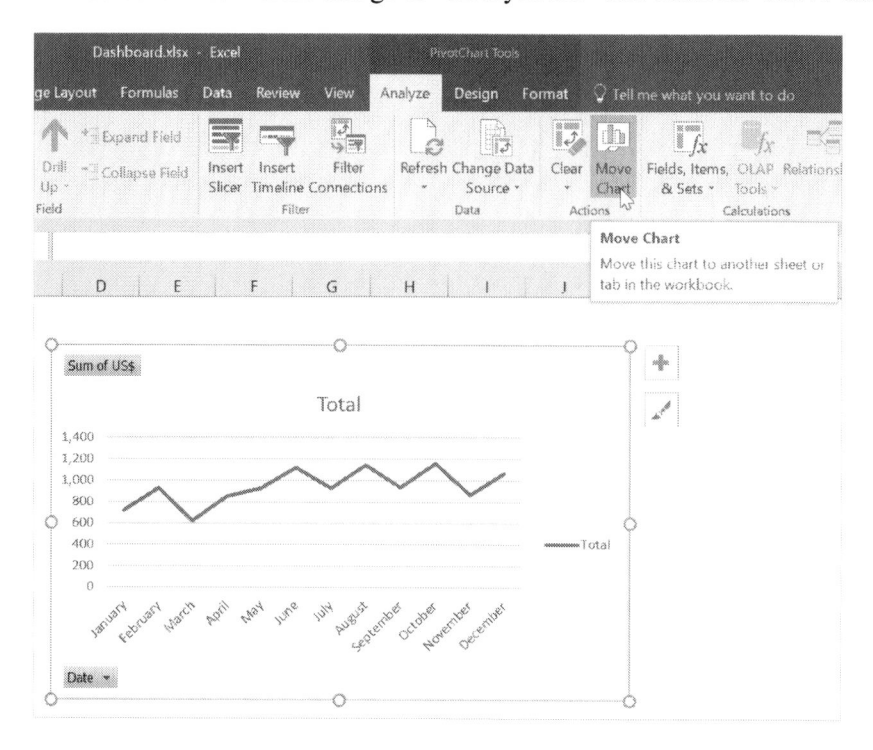

55- Select "Dashboard" and "OK".

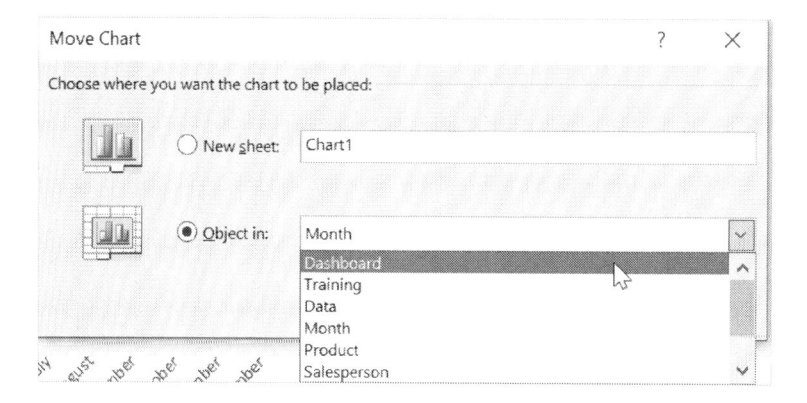

56- Select "Dashboard" and "OK".

57- Go to "Product" tab "A4".

Product

58- Right click and select "Show field list".

59- At the "Row" section insert the "Product" field.

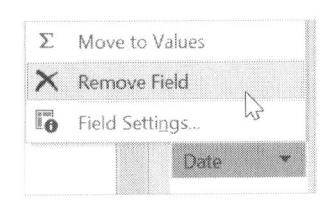

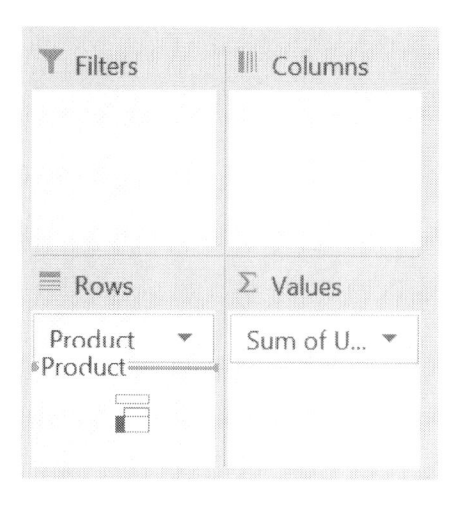

60- Go to "Analyze tab", "Tools group" and "PivotChart". Select "Clustered Column" and "OK".

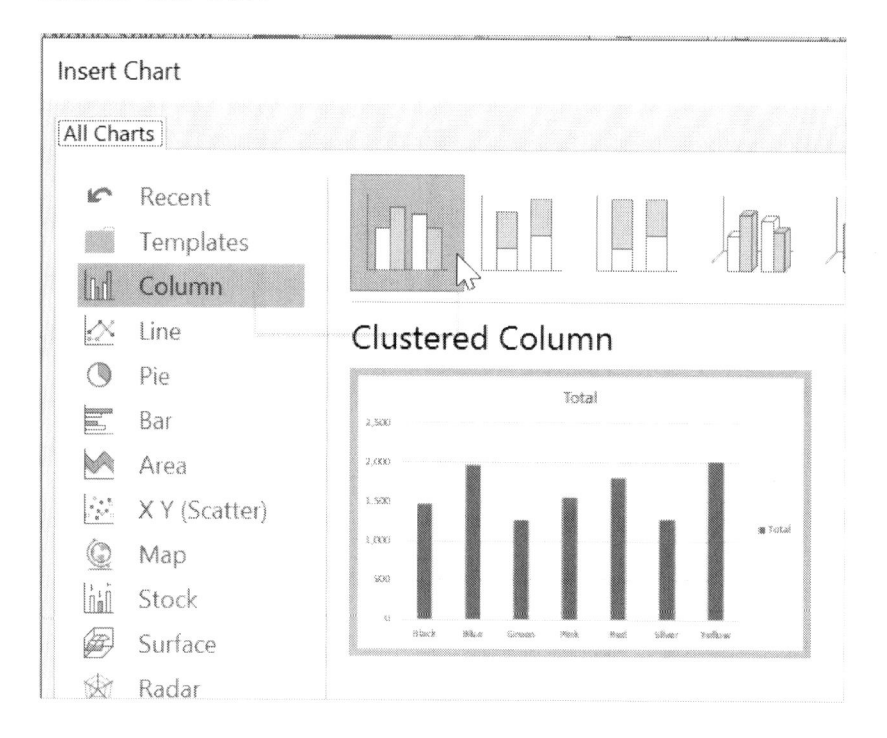

61- Right click "B4" and select "Sort Smallest to Largest".

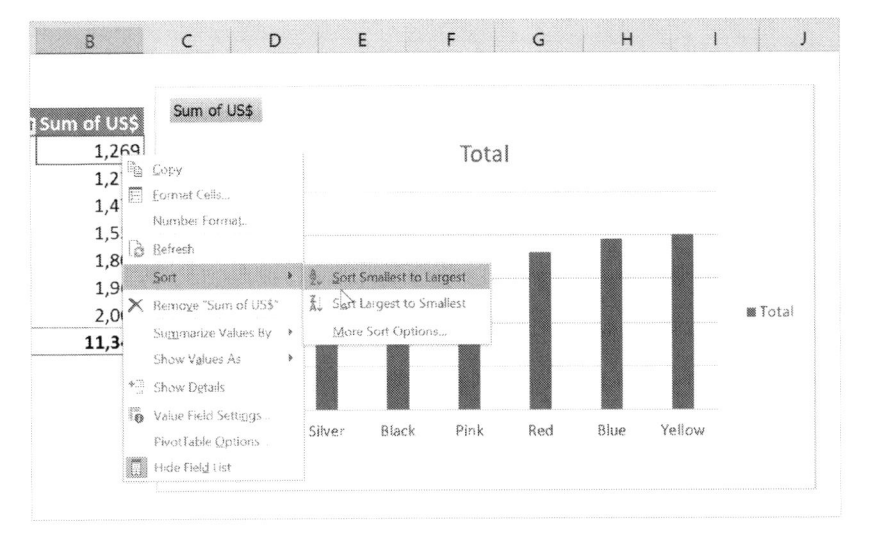

62- Right click the chart and select "Move Chart". Select Dashboard and "OK".

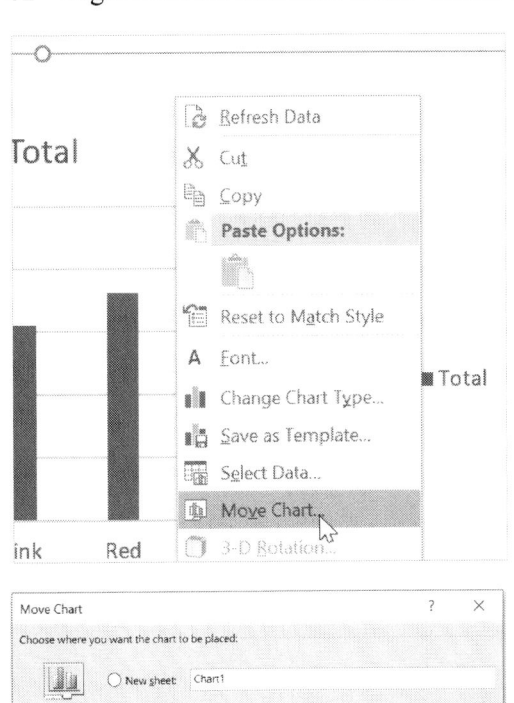

63- Go to "Salesperson" tab "A4".

64- Right click and select "Show field list".

65- At the "Row" section insert the "Salesperson" field.

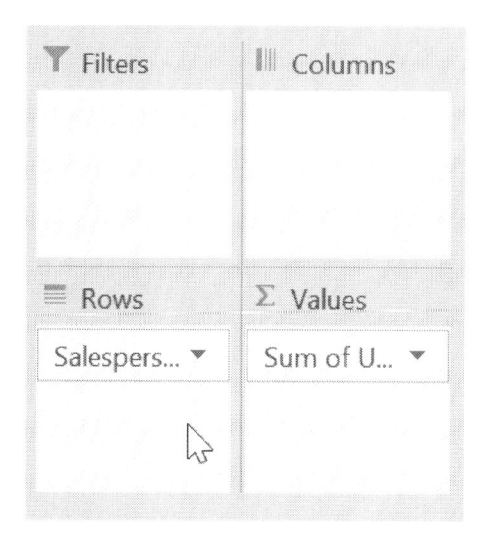

66- Go to "Analyze tab", "Tools group" and "PivotChart". Select "Clustered Bar" and "OK".

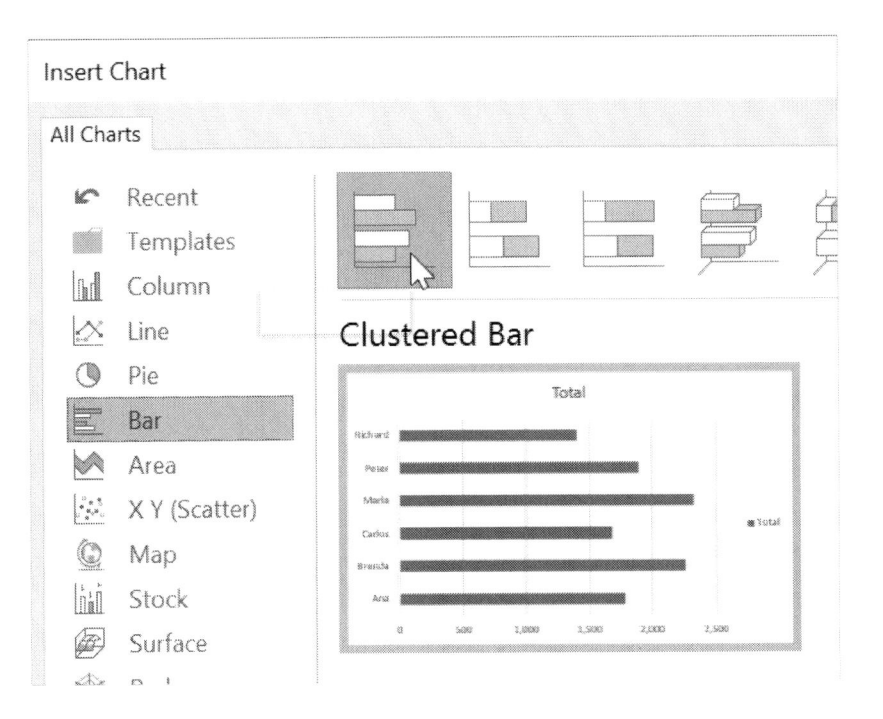

67- Right click the chart and select "Move Chart". Select Dashboard and "OK".

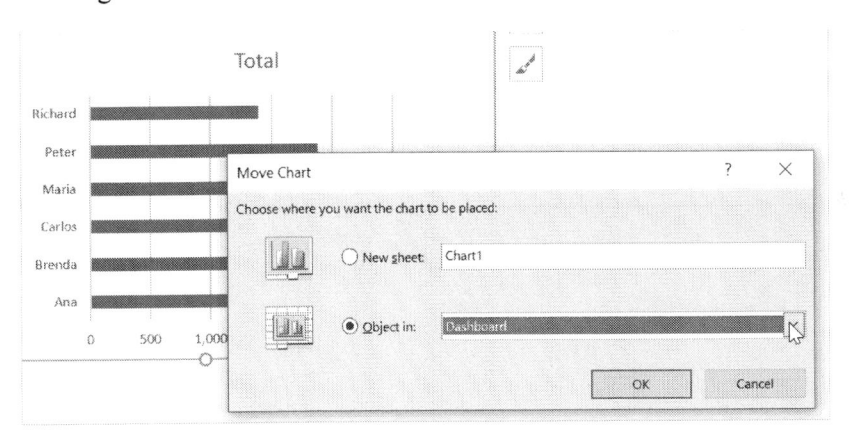

68- Go to "Region" tab "A4".

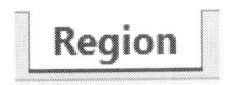

69- Right click and select "Show field list".

70- At the "Row" section insert the "Region" field.

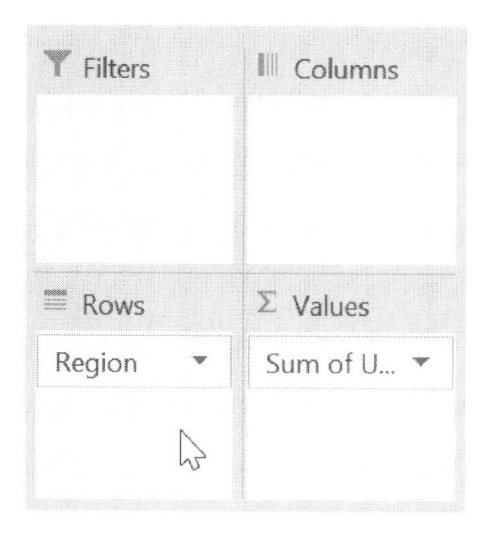

71- Go to "Analyze tab", "Tools group" and "PivotChart". Select "Radar" and "OK".

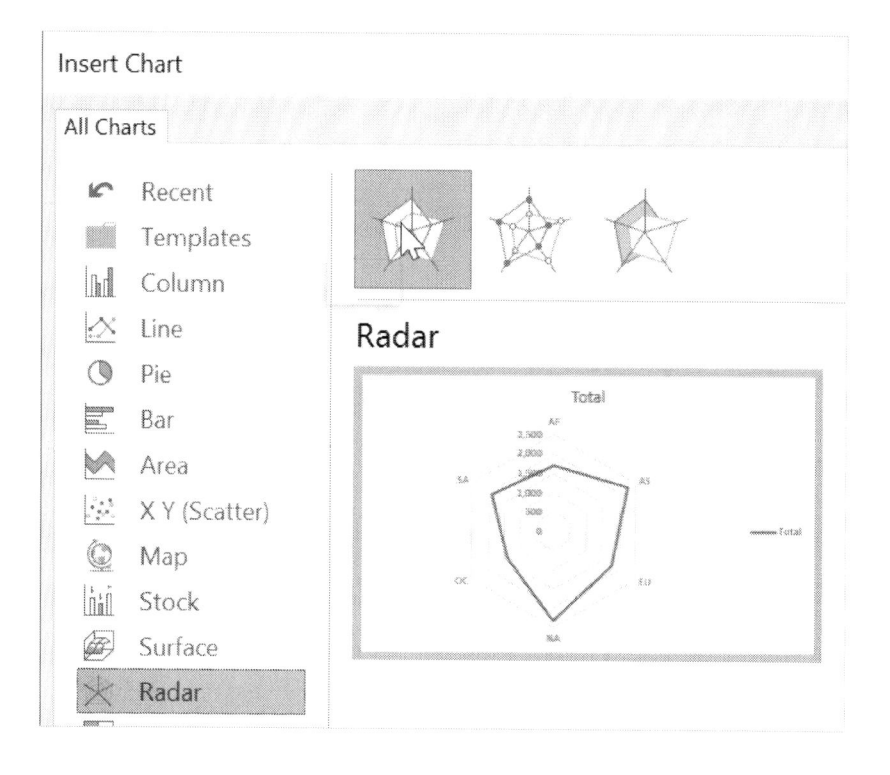

72- Right click the chart and select "Move Chart". Select Dashboard and "OK".

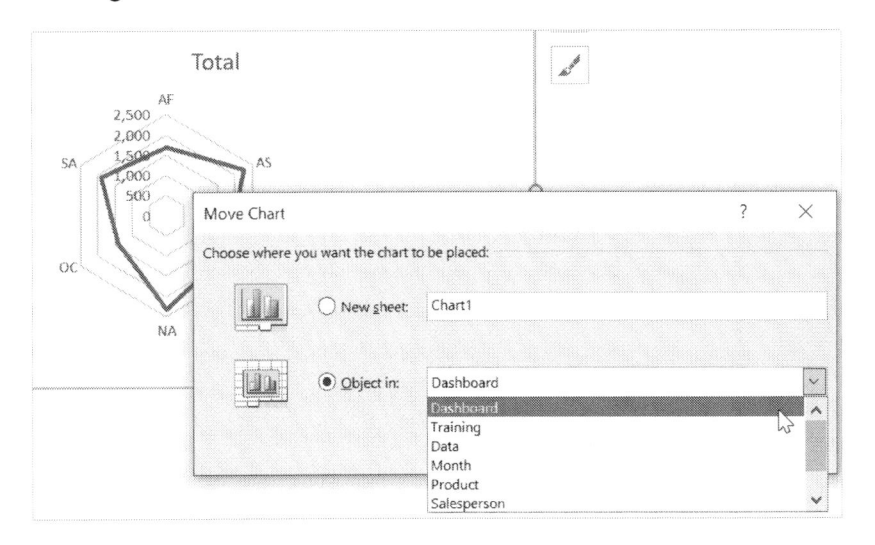

73- Go to "Dashboard" tab and move your charts as the example below (starting from row 8).

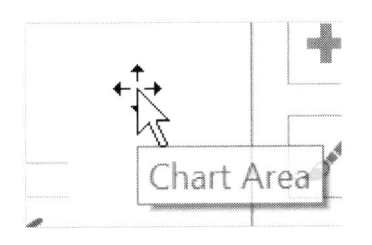

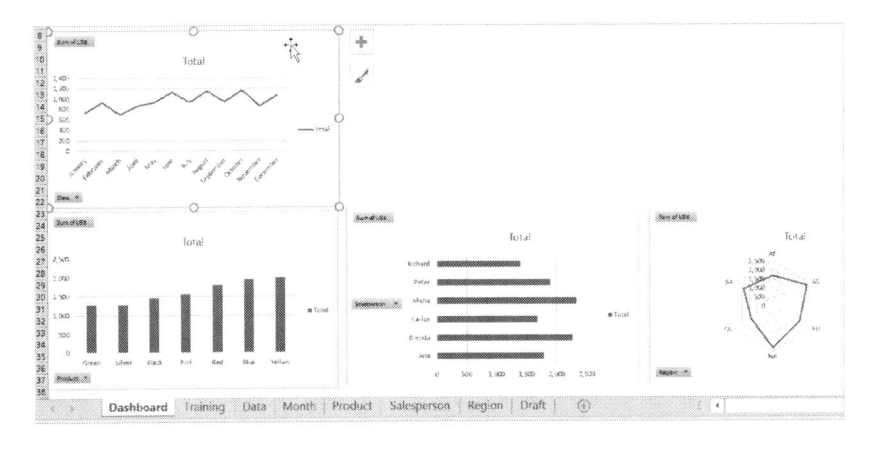

74- Select the charts and go to "Analyze tab" and click on "Field Buttons". Repeat it to each chart.

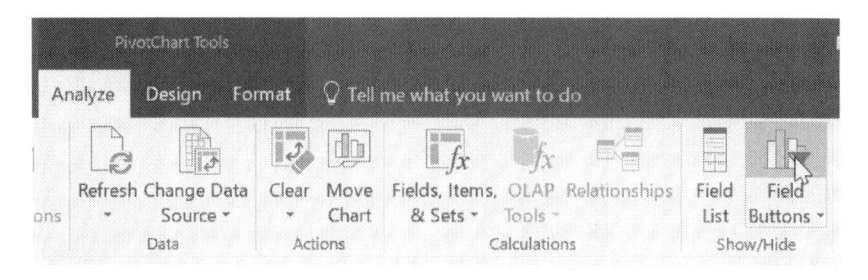

75- Select the Line chart and uncheck "Legend".

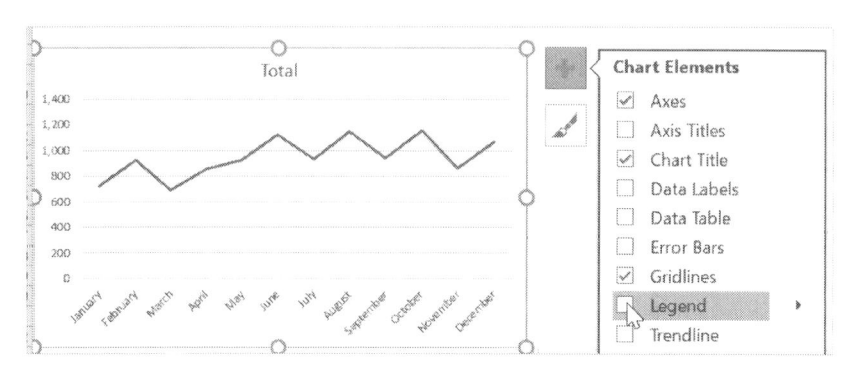

76- Double click the title and change it to "Monthly Sales".

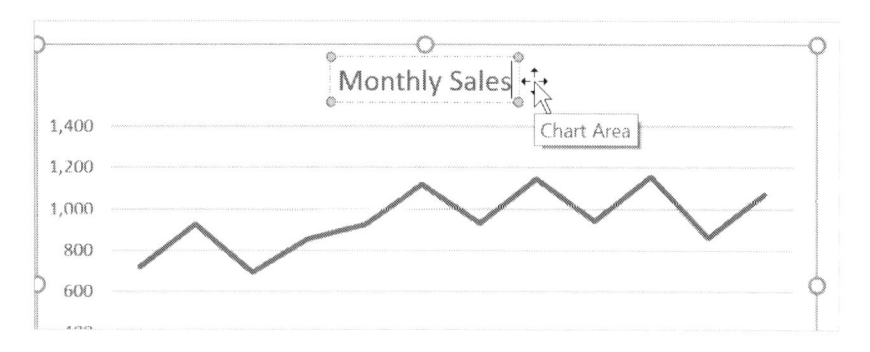

77- Change the "Legend" and "Titles" to the other charts.

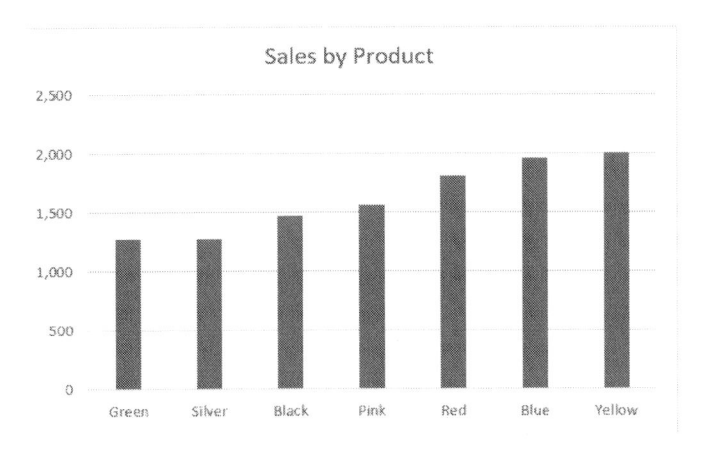

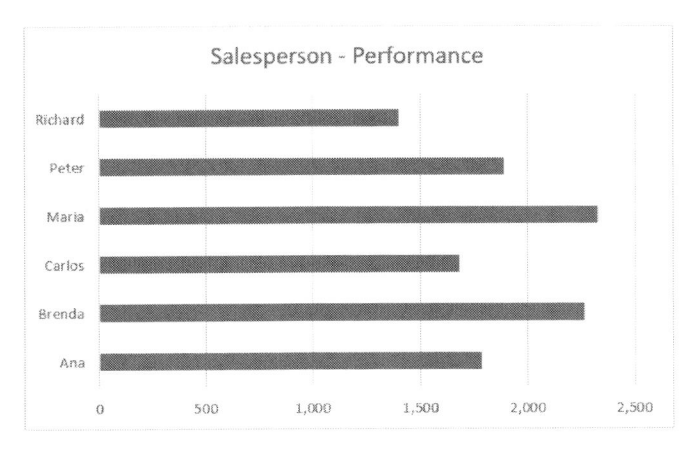

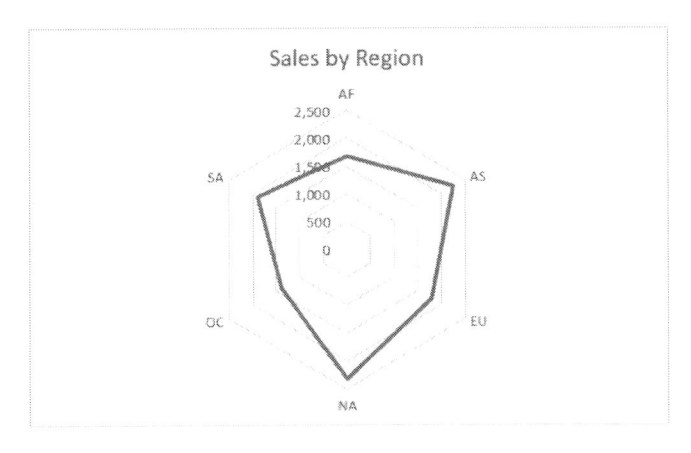

78- Select the "Sales by Product" chart and uncheck "Gridlines".

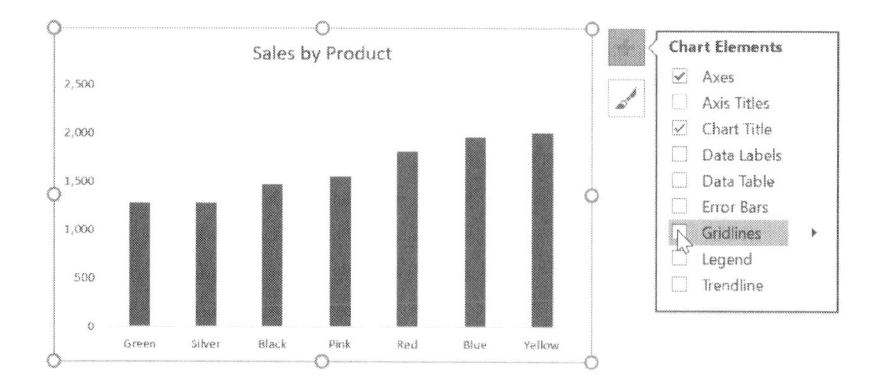

79- Right click only the bars (Data Series) and go to "Format Data Series".

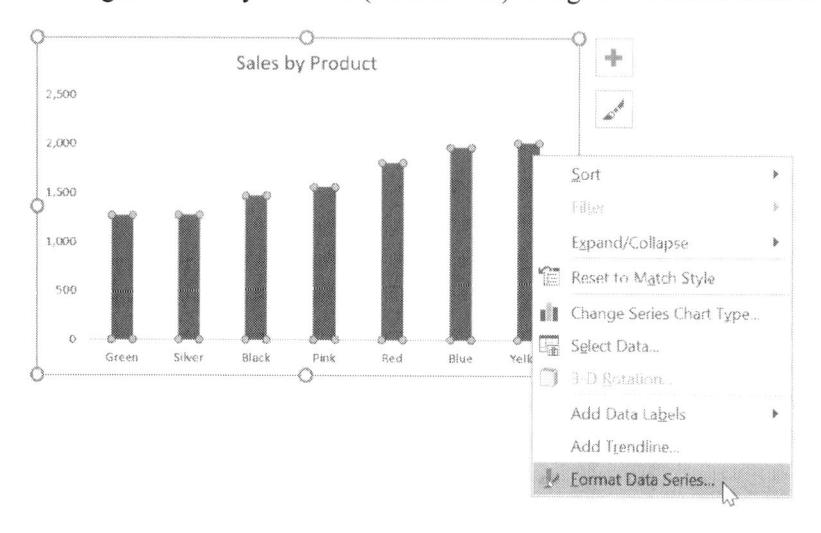

80- Go to "Series options", "Fill" and select color "Blue, Accent".

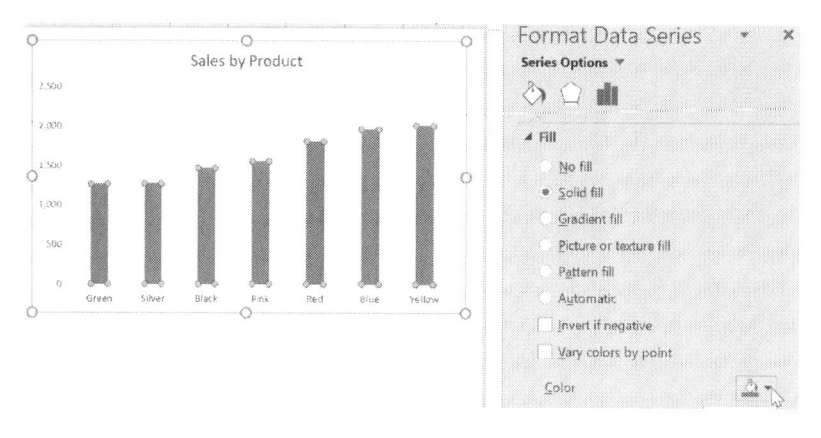

81- Select the "Salesperson" chart. Go to "Chart Elements" and check "Data Labels"

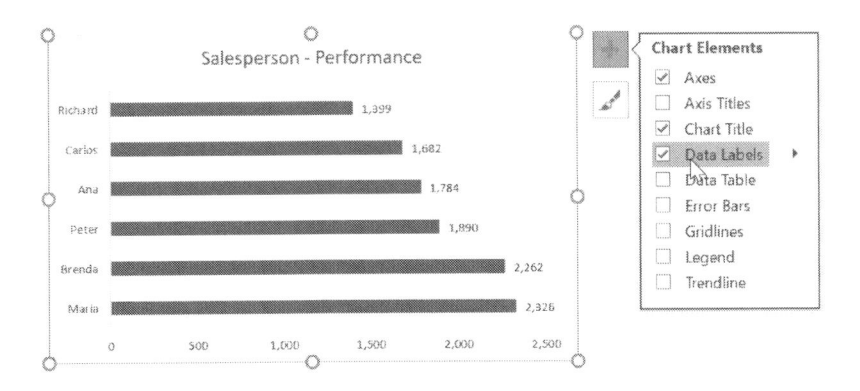

82- Go to "Axes" and check only the "Primary Vertical".
Note: As you already have the data in your labels is a good practice to avoid duplications by removing the horizontal numbers.

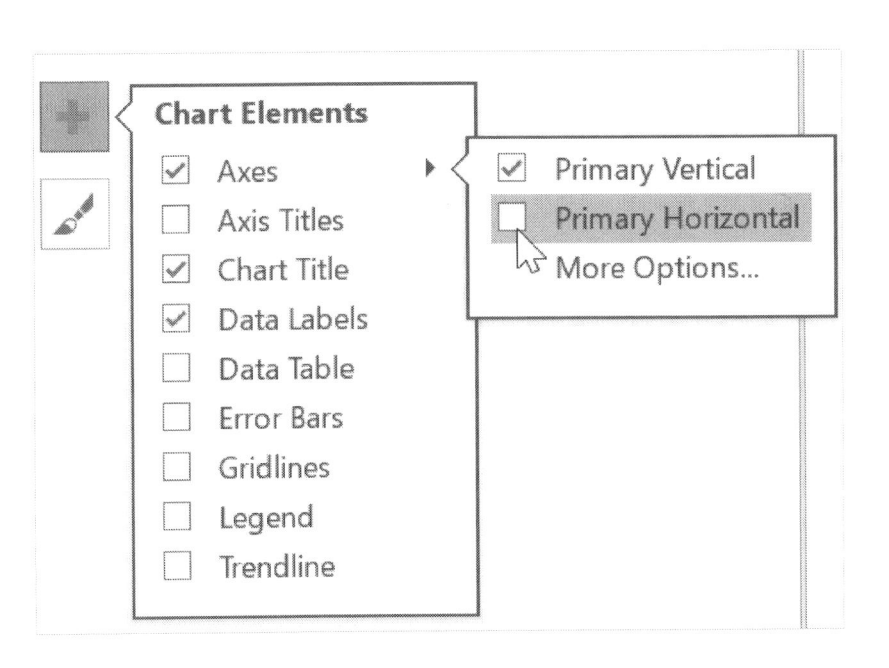

83- Select the bars (Data Series) and change the color by going to "Format tab", "Shape Fill" and select "Blue, Accent)

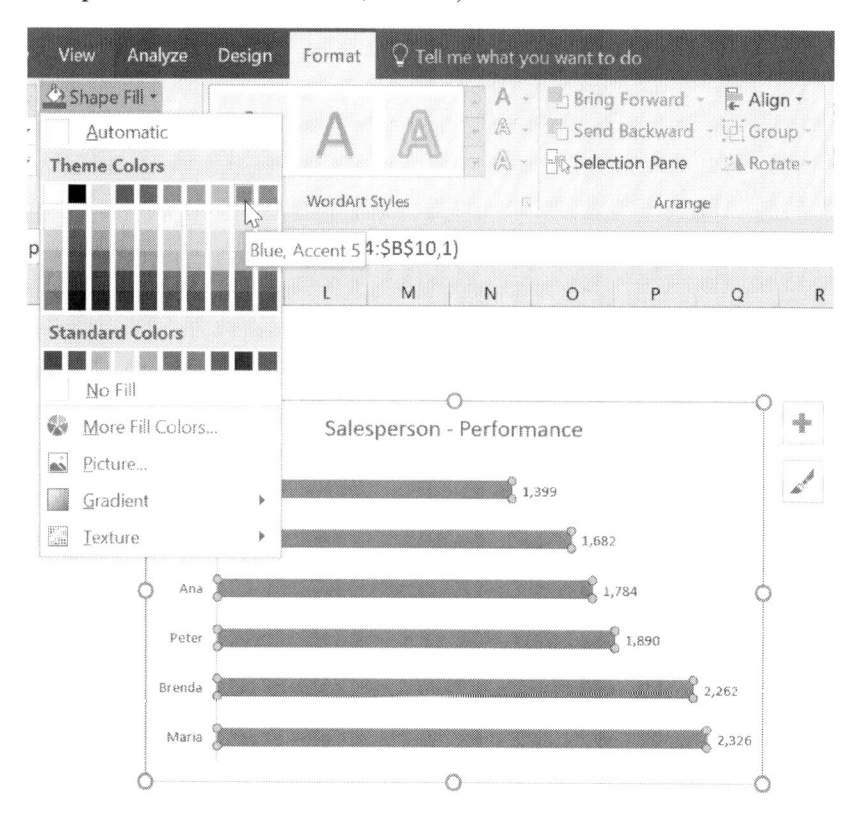

84- Select "Sales by Region" chart and uncheck Axes.

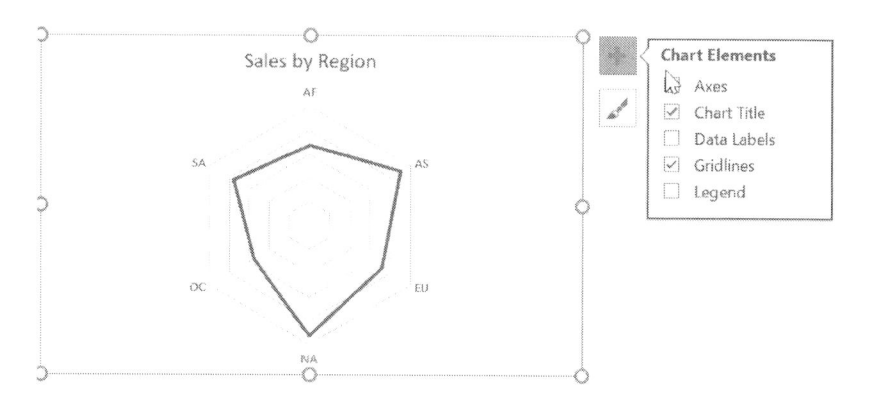

85- Select the chart and go to "Format tab", "Size group" and set the Height and Width as image below. Do the same to the other charts.

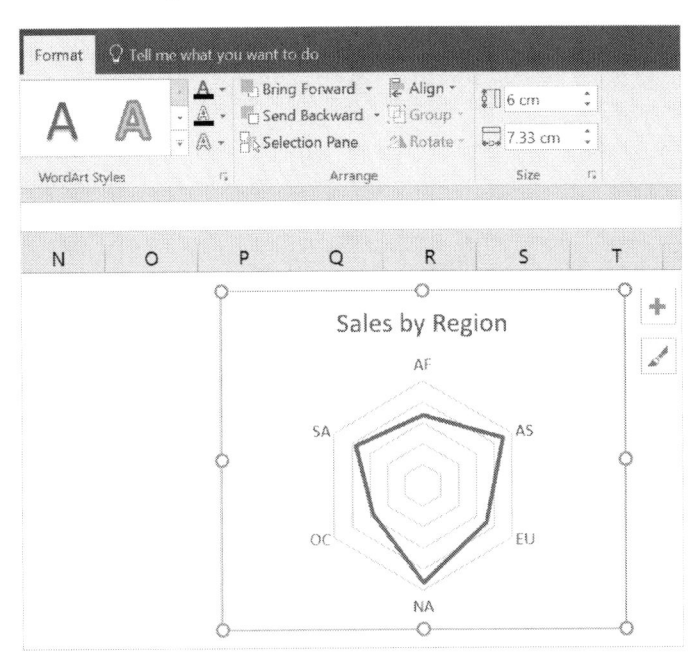

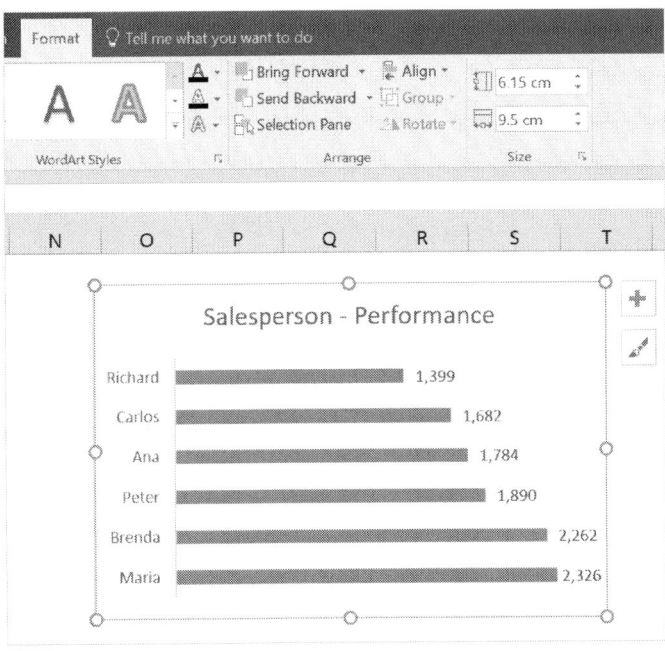

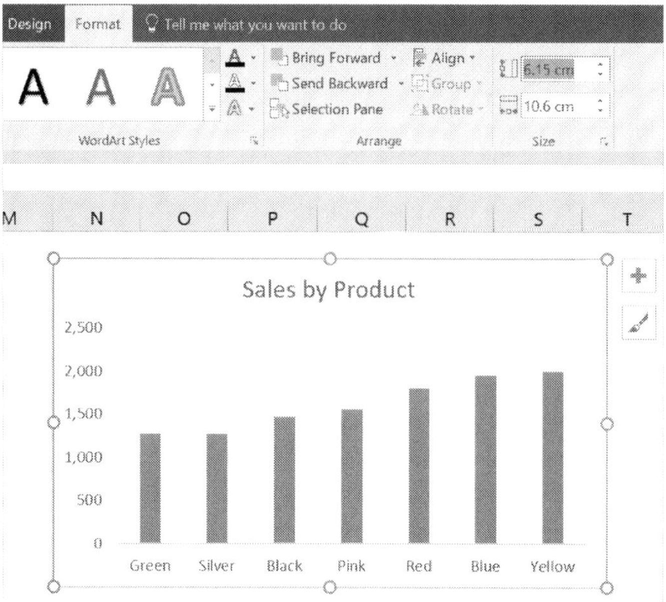
Design
Format
Tell me what you want to do
Bring Forward
Send Backward
Selection Pane
Align
Group
Rotate
6.15 cm
10.6 cm
WordArt Styles
Arrange
Size
M N O P Q R S T
Sales by Product
2,500
2,000
1,500
1,000
500
0
Green
Silver
Black
Pink
Red
Blue
Yellow

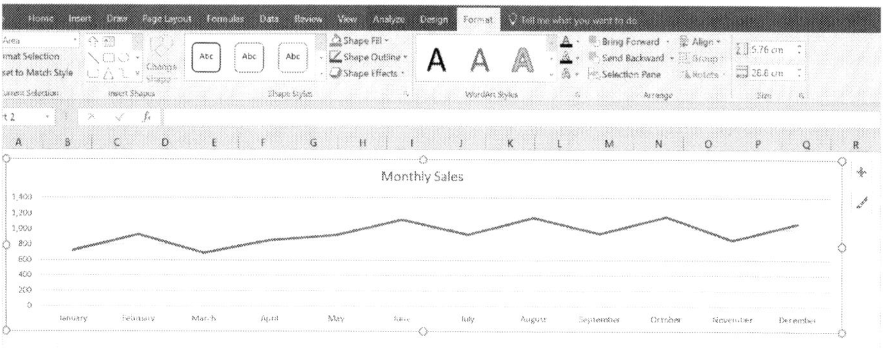
Home Insert Draw Page Layout Formulas Data Review View Analyze Design Format
Tell me what you want to do
Format Selection
Reset to Match Style
Current Selection
Insert Shapes
Change Shape
Abc
Abc
Abc
Shape Fill
Shape Outline
Shape Effects
Shape Styles
WordArt Styles
Bring Forward
Send Backward
Selection Pane
Align
Group
Rotate
Arrange
5.76 cm
26.8 cm
Size
A B C D E F G H I J K L M N O P Q R
Monthly Sales
1,400
1,200
1,000
800
600
400
200
0
January
February
March
April
May
June
July
August
September
October
November
December

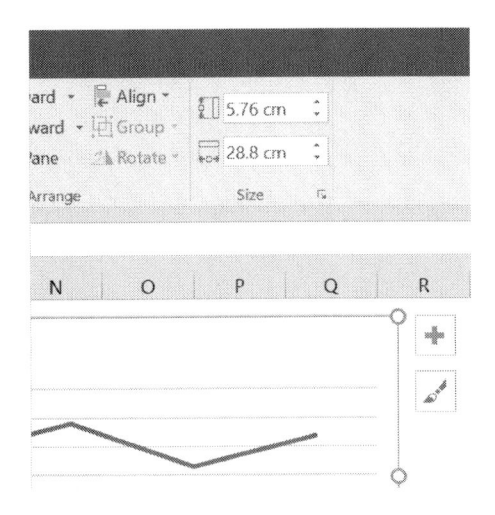

86- Go to "Monthly Sales" chart and right click the line. Select "Format Data Series".

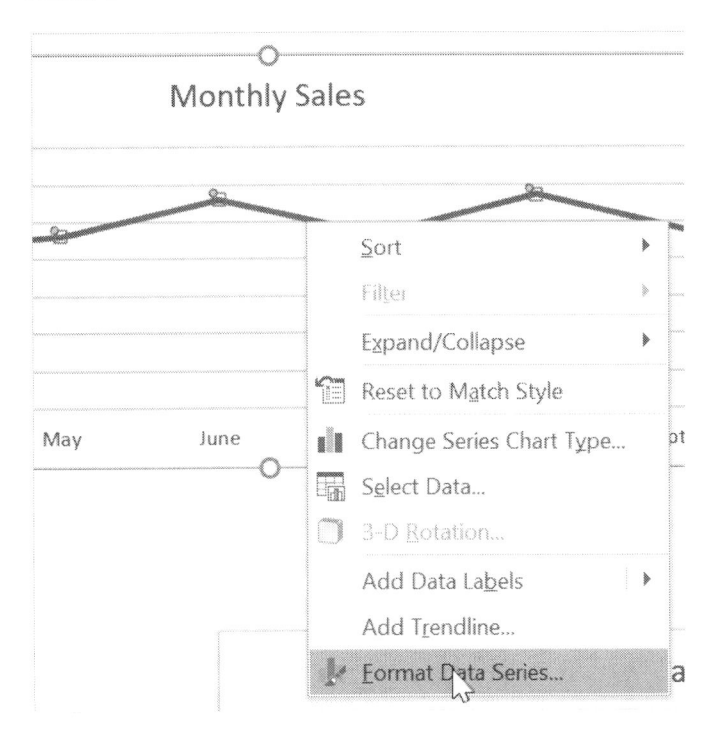

87- Go to "Series Options", "Line", check "Solid line" and change the color to "Blue, accent".

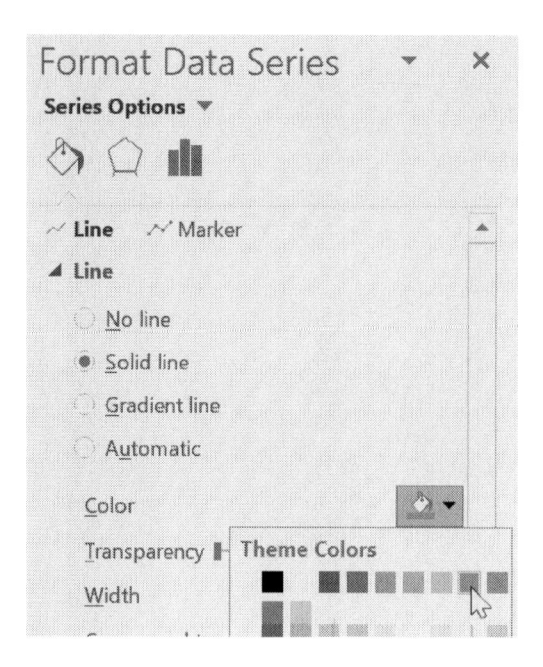

88- Change "Width" to 4pt.

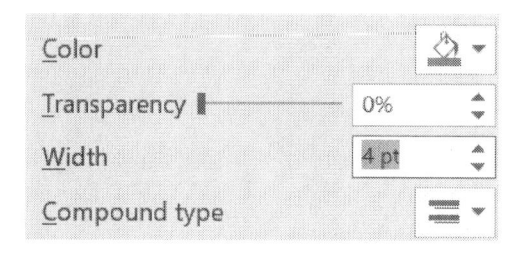

89- Go to "Markers", "Marker Options", change the configuration to the same below (Type and Size).

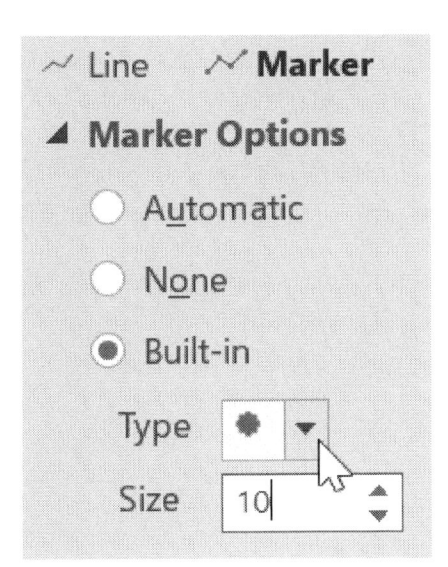

90- Go to "Fill", select "Solid fill" and change the color to white.

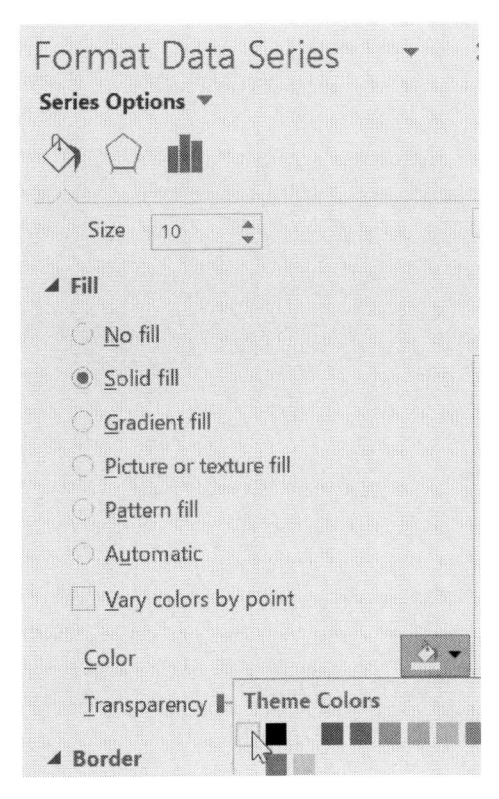

91- Change the markers line to solid, "Blue, accent" and "Width" 4.

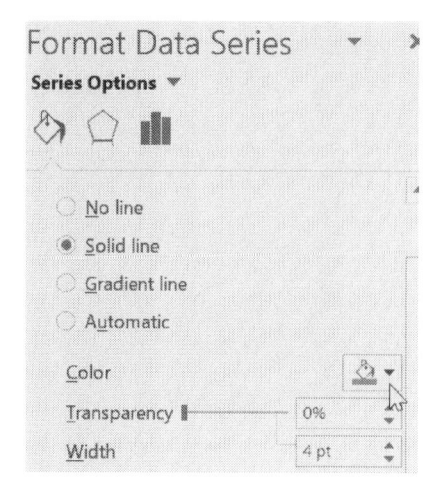

92- Click on the left corner to select the whole sheet.

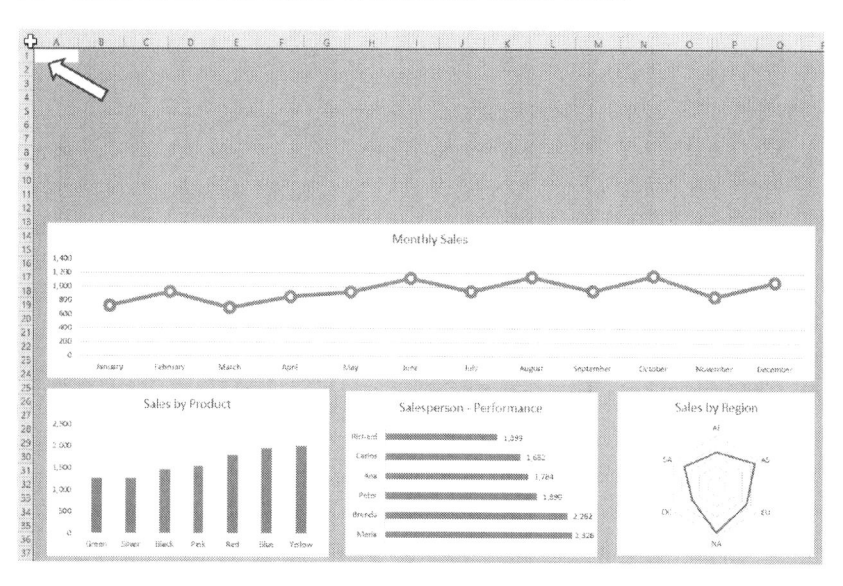

93- Change the cells color to "Light gray".

Theme Colors

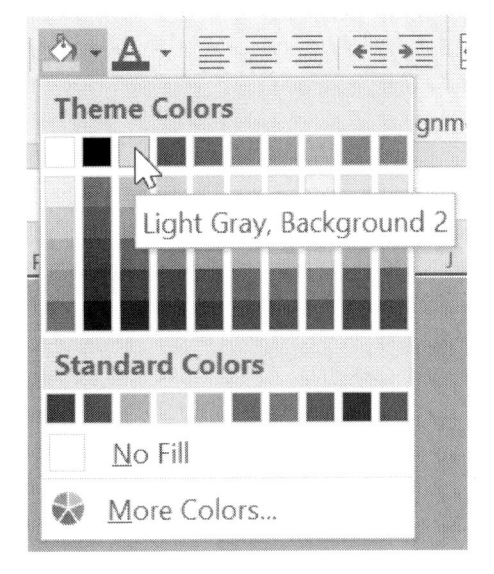

Light Gray, Background 2

Standard Colors

No Fill

More Colors...

5. Slicers and Timeline

94- Select the "Sales by Product" chart, go to "Insert tab", "Filters group", and click on "Time Line".

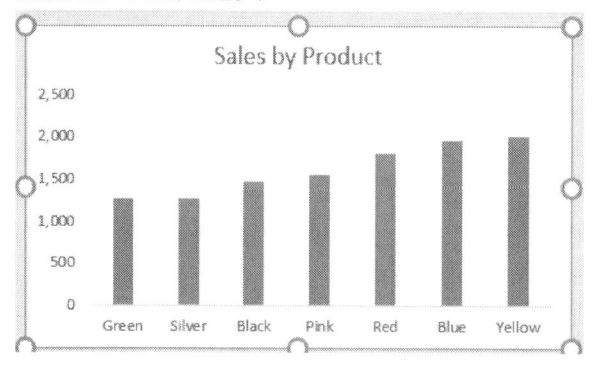

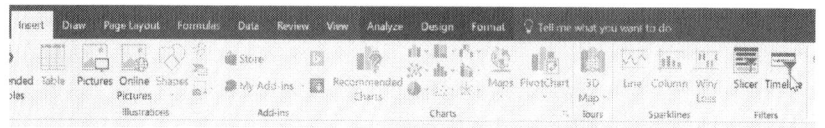

95- Check the date field that will be filtered "Date" and "OK".

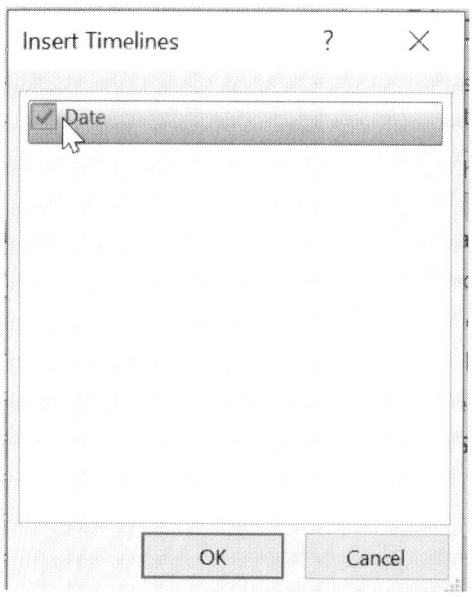

96- Click on the new timeline, go to "Options tab", "Timeline Styles group" and select "Light Blue".

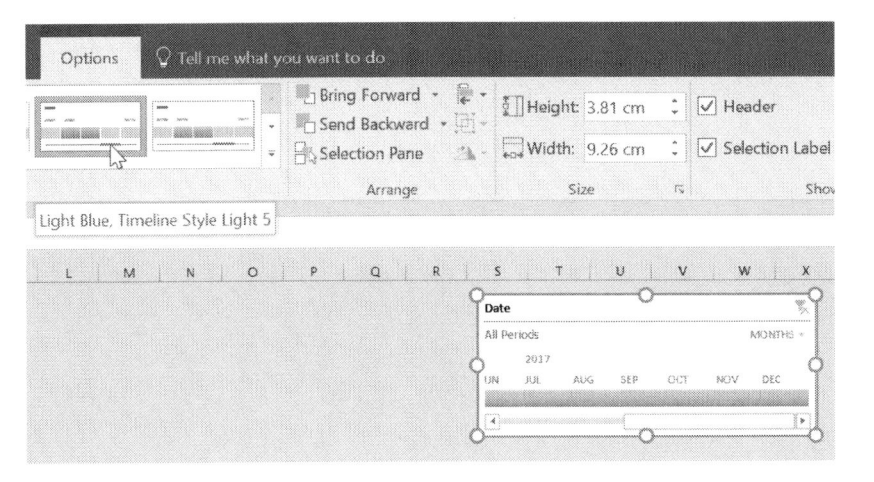

97- Now, click on "Report Connections" to connect charts to the timeline.

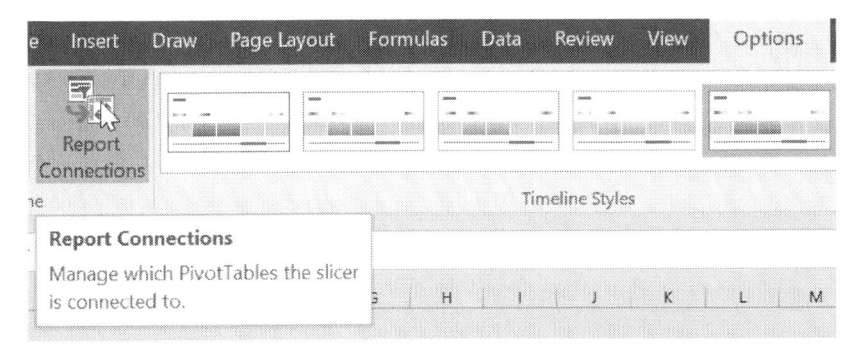

98- Check "pvtMonth" and "pvtSalesperson", then "OK".

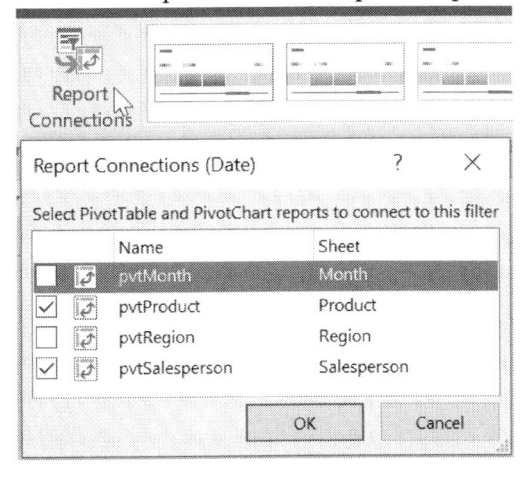

99- You can filter by selecting specific range dates to detail your data. To clear the filter just click the button at top right.

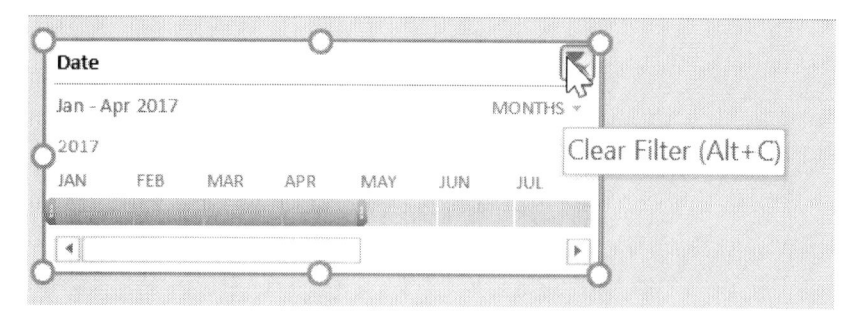

100- Select the "Monthly Sales" chart, go to "Insert tab", "Filters group", and click on "Slicer".

101- Check the group field that will be filtered, "Region" and "OK".

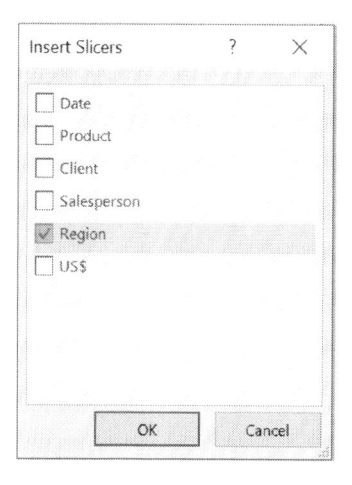

102- Check "pvtMonth", "pvtProduct" and "pvtSlesperson" then "OK".

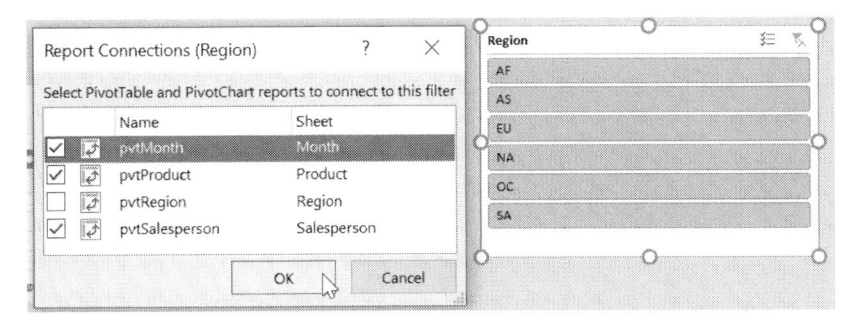

103- Select the "Sales by Product" chart, go to "Insert tab", "Filters group", and create a new "Slicer". Check "Salesperson" and "OK".

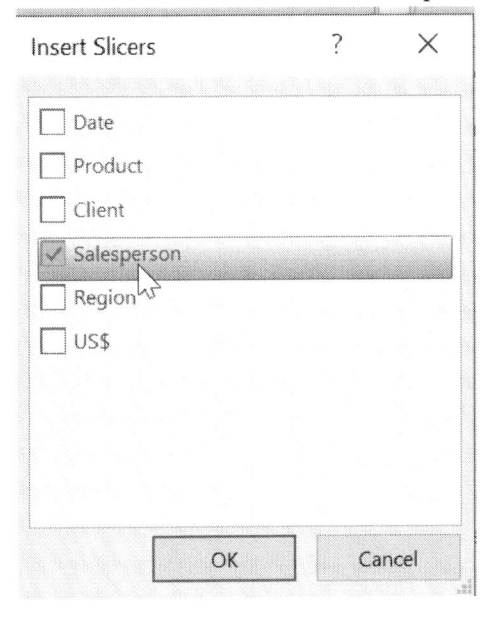

104- Check "pvtMonth" and "pvtProduct" then "OK".

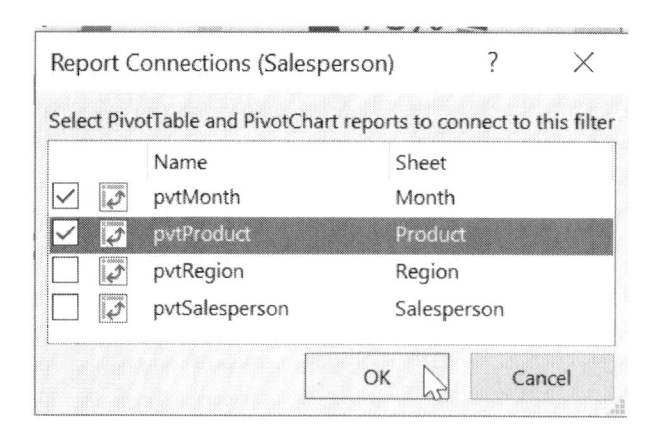

		Name	Sheet
✓		pvtMonth	Month
✓		pvtProduct	Product
		pvtRegion	Region
		pvtSalesperson	Salesperson

105- Select the filters and go to "Options tab", "Size group" and set the Height and Width as images below.

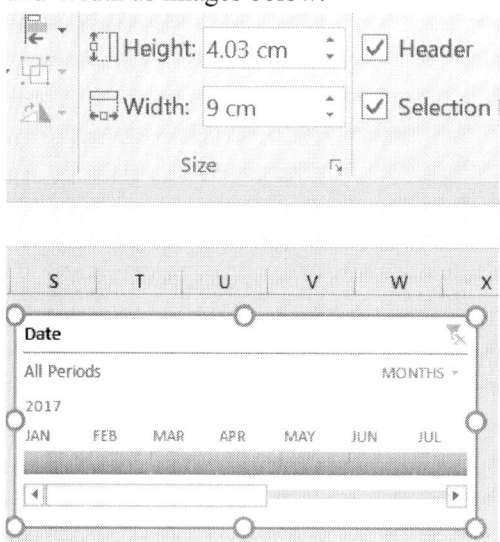

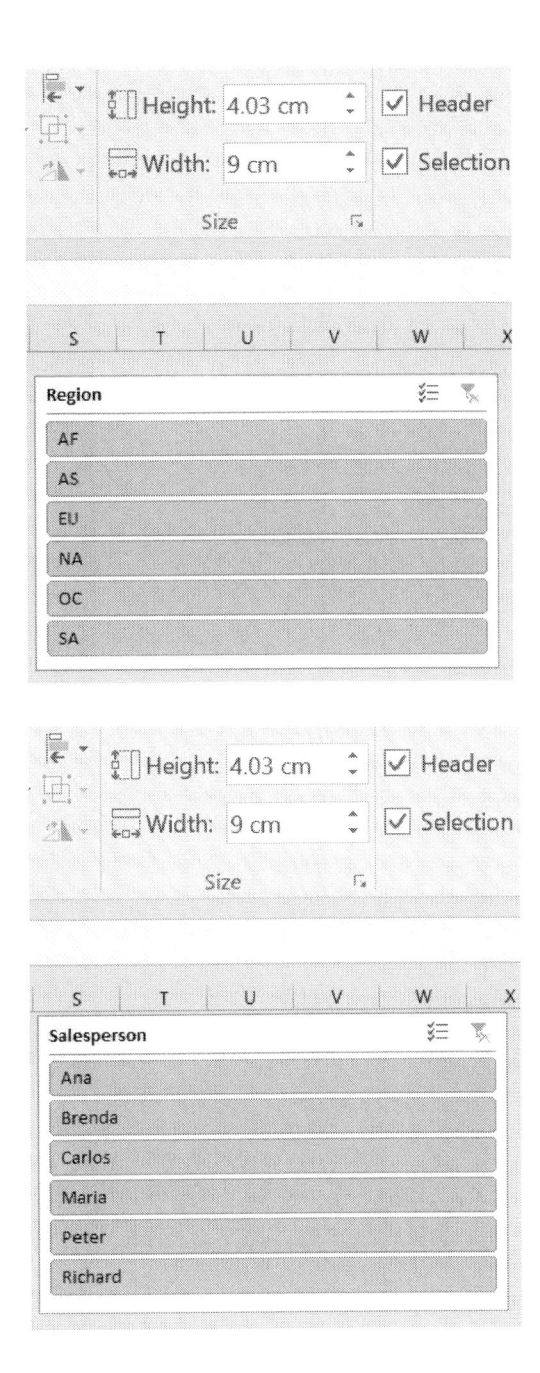

106- Select each Slicer and go to "Options". Change the "Slicer Styles" to "Light Blue".

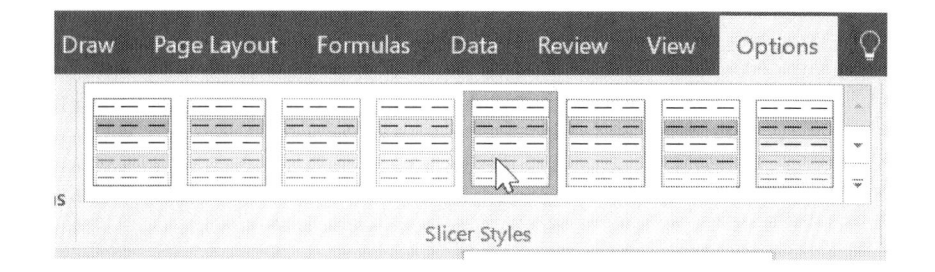

107- Move the items to look like image below.

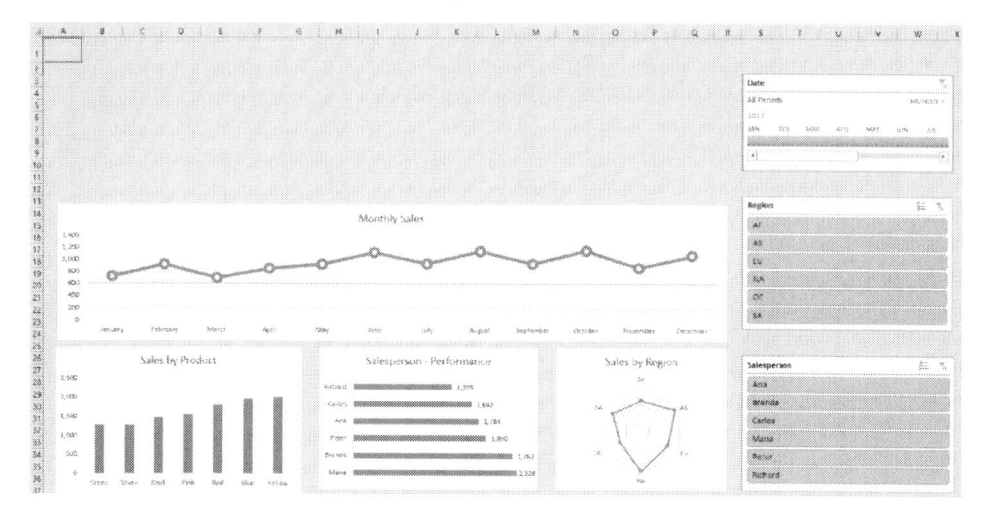

6. Doughnut Charts and Links

108- Go to "Data" Tab.

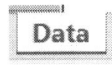

109- Select range I3:I4.

	H	I
1	Sales Target	
2	Target	15,000.00
3	Sales	11,342.80
4	Gap	3,657.20

110- Go to "Insert tab" and insert a "Doughnut Chart".

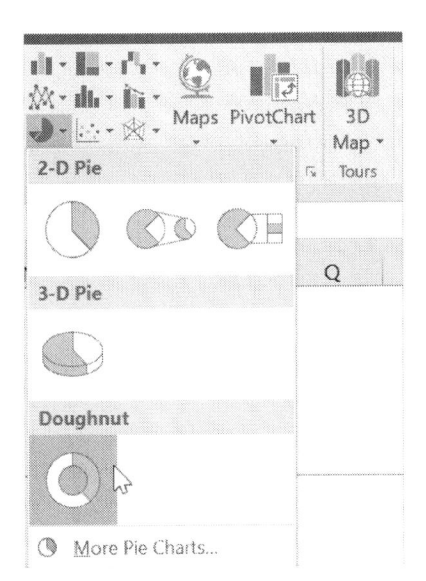

111- Click on the chart, go to "Chart Elements" and check only "Chart Title".

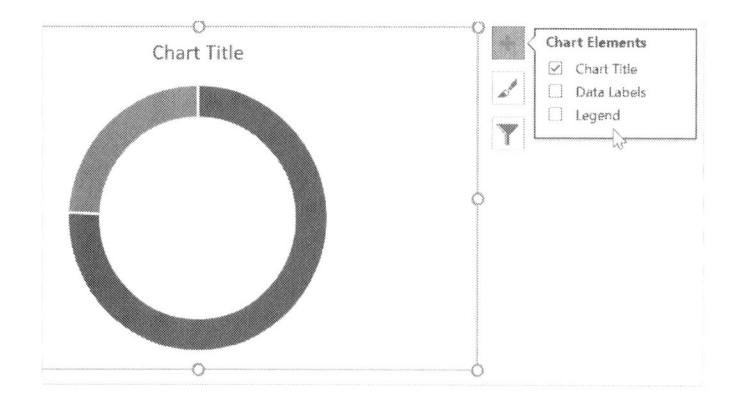

112- Right click the series and go to "Format Data Series".

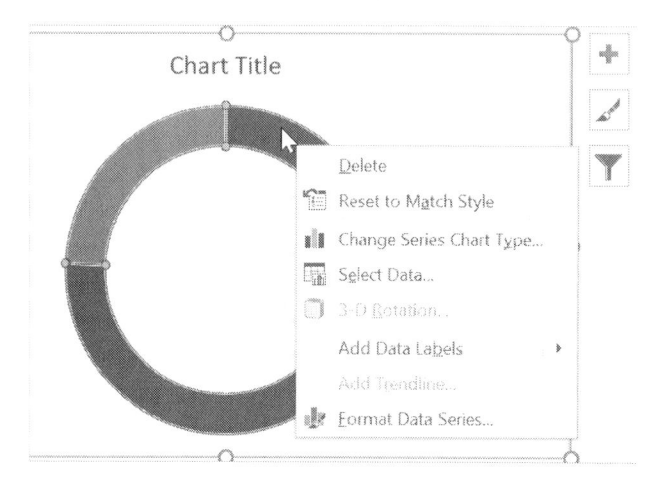

Go to "Series Options" and set the "Angle" to 180° and "Size" to 65%.

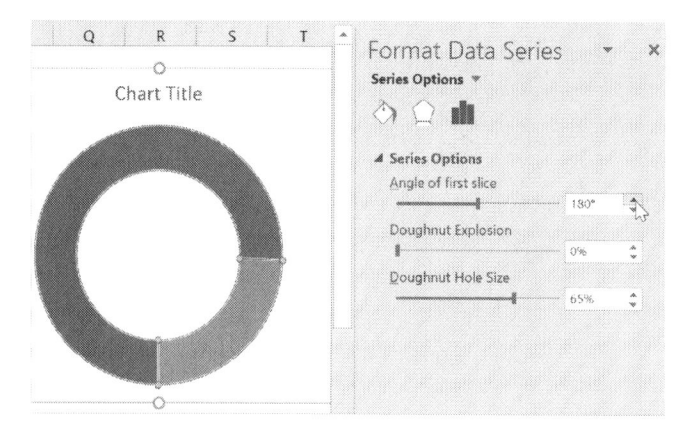

113- Double click the larger area, after selecting only it, right click and select "Format Data Point". Then, change the colours as image below.

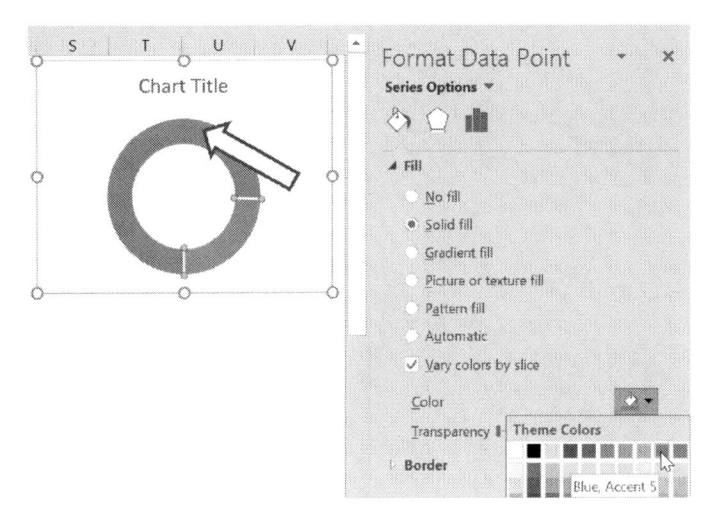

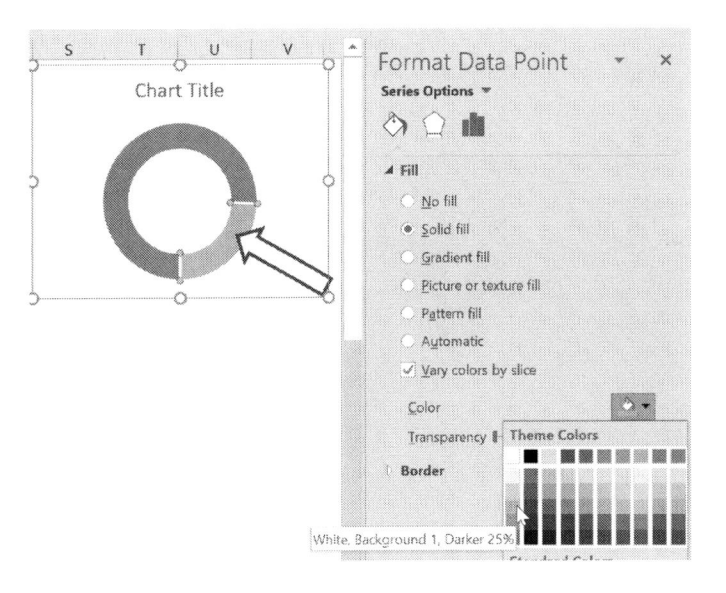

114- Select the new chart and go to "Insert tab", "Text Box".

115- Click over the chart to insert the new text box

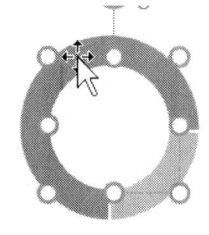

116- With the text box selected, go to "Formula Bar" and type =$I$5 and "Enter", to link the data to the text box.

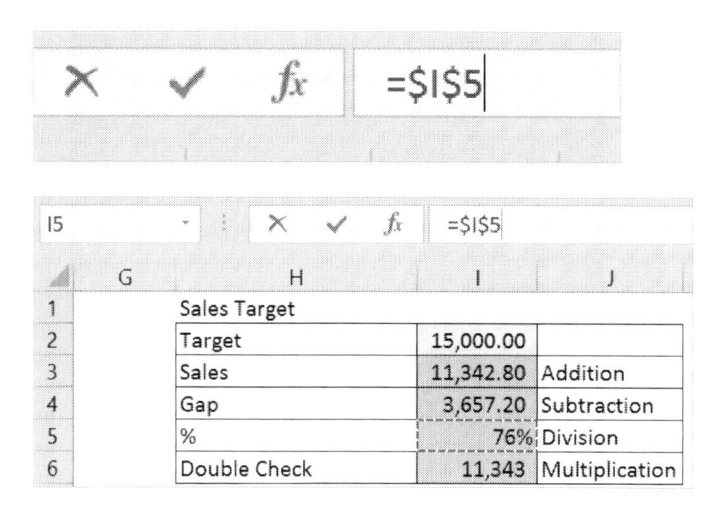

117- Change the title to "Sales Target" Set the font as "Calibri", size 28.

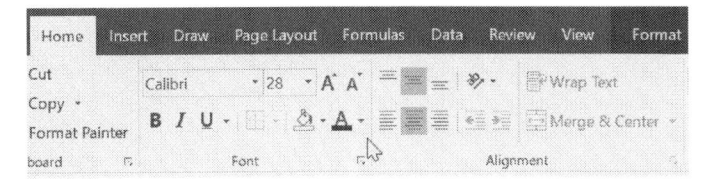

118- Copy and paste the doughnut chart to have four charts.

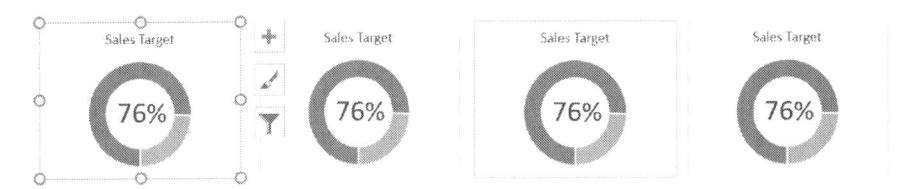

119- Change their titles to "Sales Target", "Market Share", "Marketing Budget" and, "Customer Satisfaction".

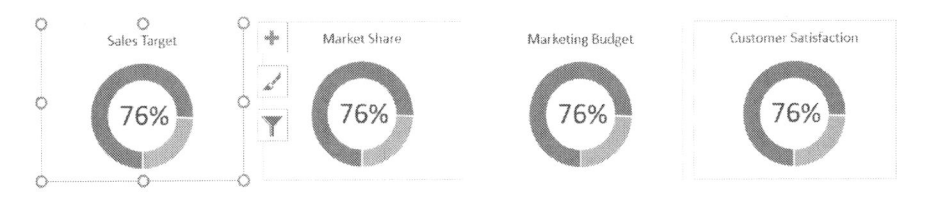

120- Right click the "Market Share" chart and click on "Select Data".

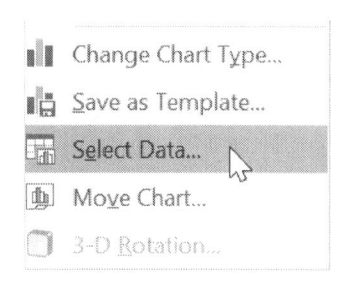

- Change Chart Type...
- Save as Template...
- **Select Data...**
- Move Chart...
- 3-D Rotation...

121- Set the "Chart data range" to =Data!$I$10:$I$11

Select Data Source

Chart data range: =Data!$I$10:$I$11

122- To "Marketing Budget" chart, set the "Chart data range" to =Data!$I$15:$I$16

Select Data Source

Chart data range: =Data!$I$15:$I$16

123- To "Customer Satisfaction" chart, set the "Chart data range" to =Data!$I$21:$I$22

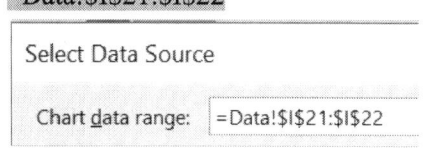

Select Data Source

Chart data range: =Data!$I$21:$I$22

124- Set the text box links inside of each chart as figures below.

Market Share:

f_x =Data!$I$10

Market Share
45%
Series 1 Point
Value: 55% (55

Marketing Budget:

=Data!$I$17

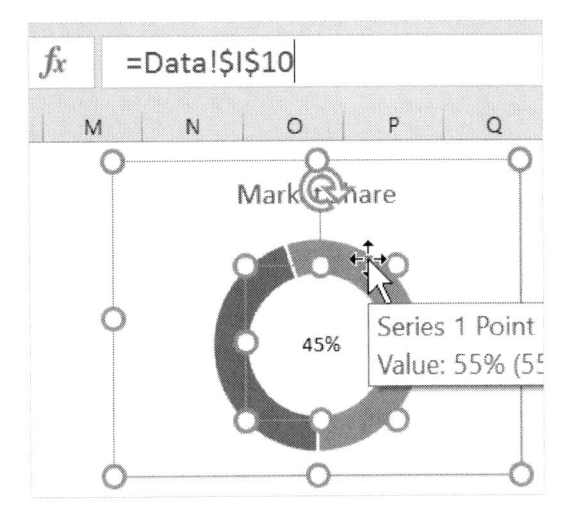

Marketing Budget
76%
TextBox 2

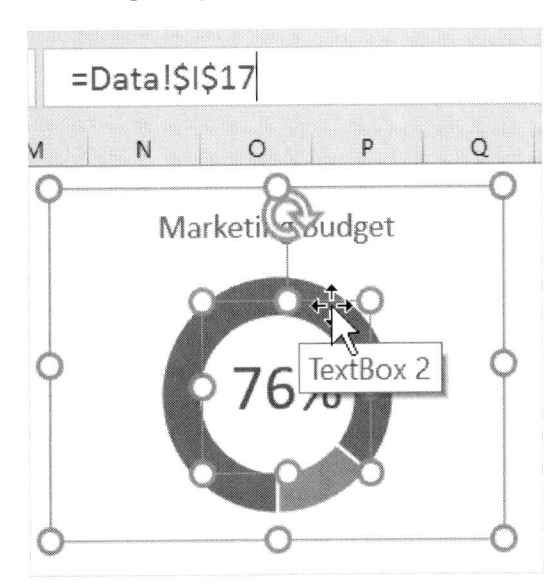

Customer Satisfaction

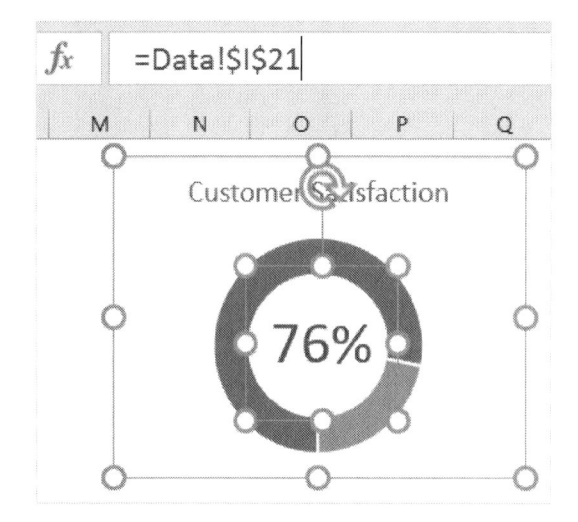

125- Change the chart colors as below:
Market Share: Green, Accent 6.
Marketing Budget: Orange, Accent 2.
Customer Satisfaction: Purple

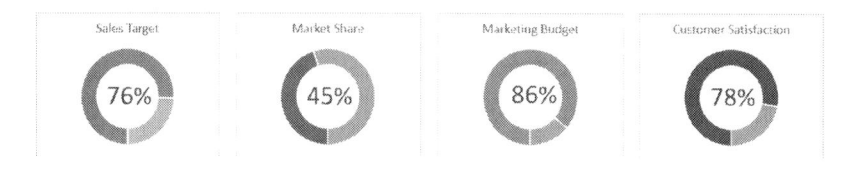

126- Select each chart and move to the Dashboard tab.

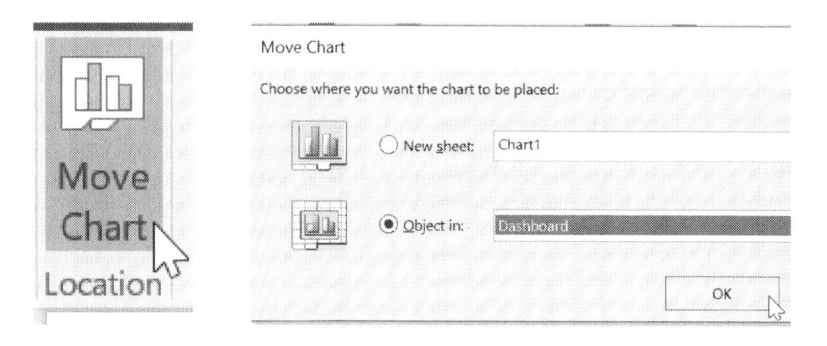

127- Go to the "Dashboard" tab.

128- Organize the charts as below:

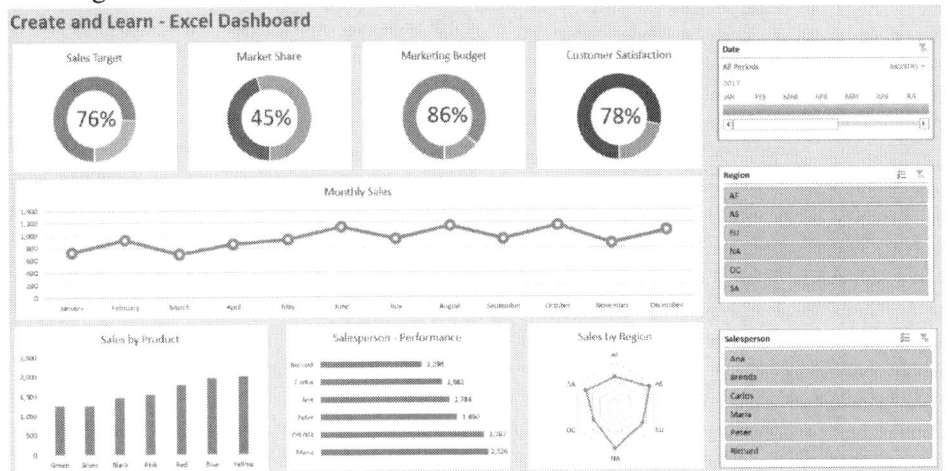

7. Aligning Charts and objects

129- Select the charts at left by holding "Shift" and clicking on each.

130- Go to "Format tab", "Arrange group", and select "Align Left".

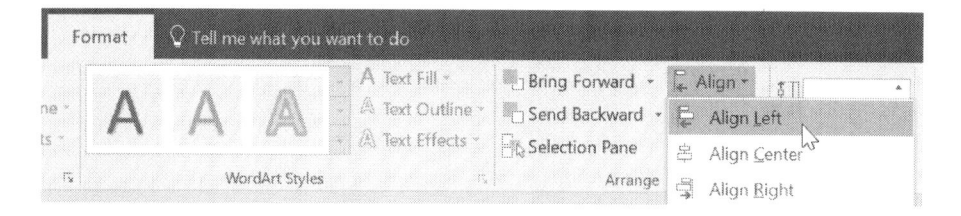

131- Select the Doughnut charts and click on "Align Top"

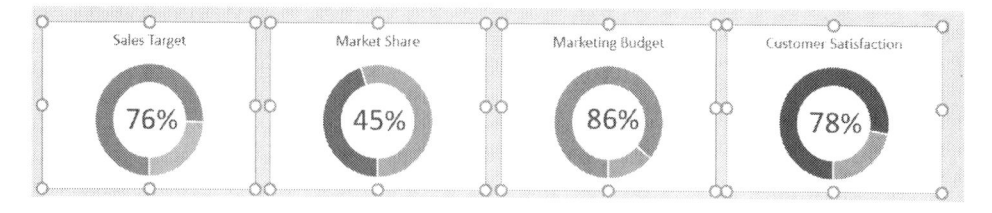

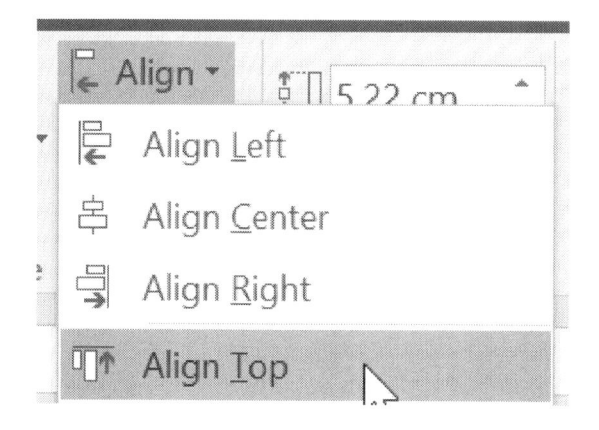

132- Select the charts at right and click on "Align Right".

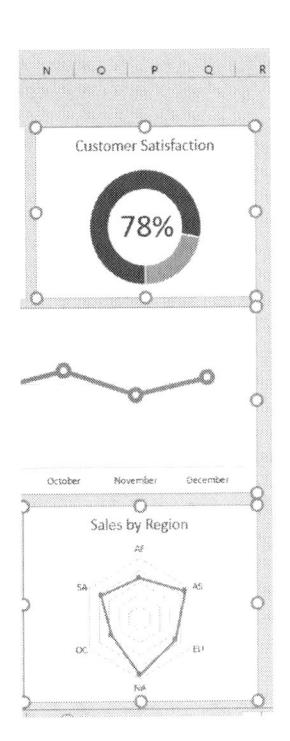

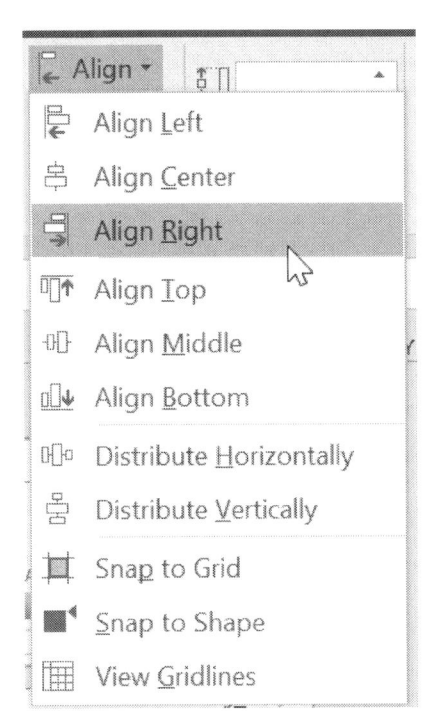

133- You can play with the alignments on the charts and filters. Try to have a result like below.

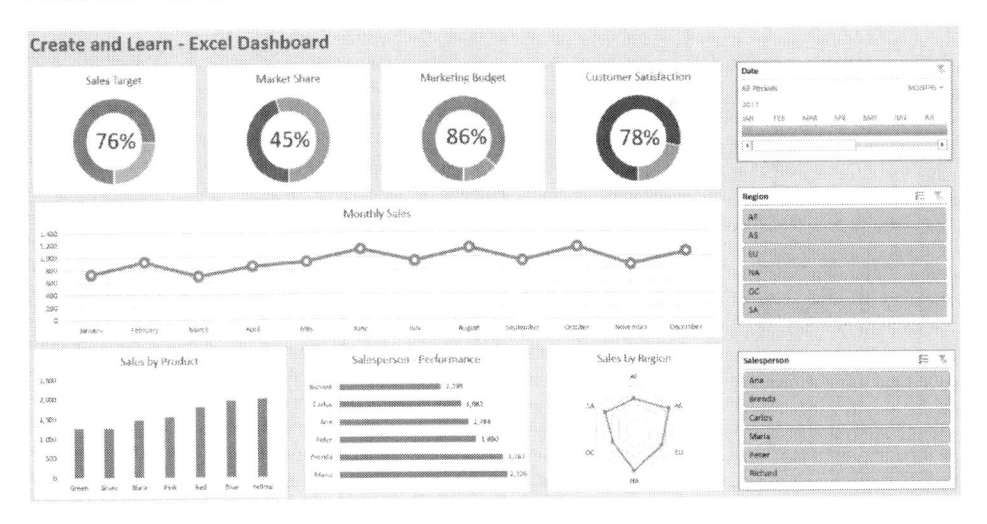

8. Printing setup

134- Go to "View tab", "Workbook Views group" and click on "Page Break Preview".

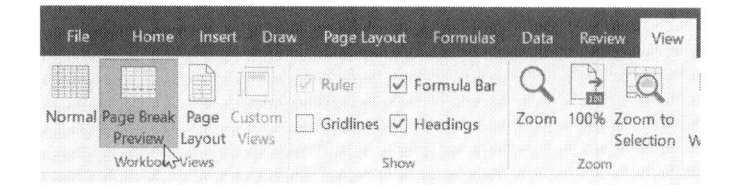

135- Move the print borders (blue borders, dashed also) to fit only the dashboard inside the print area.

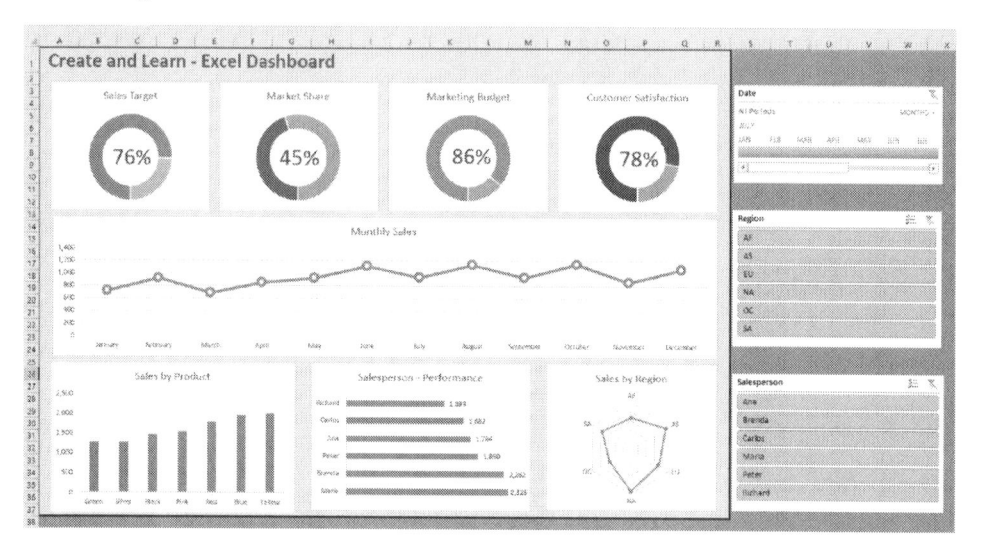

136- Once finished click on "Normal".

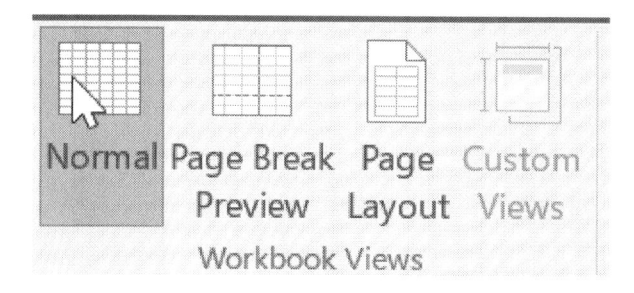

137- Go to "Page Layout tab" and click on "Page Setup".

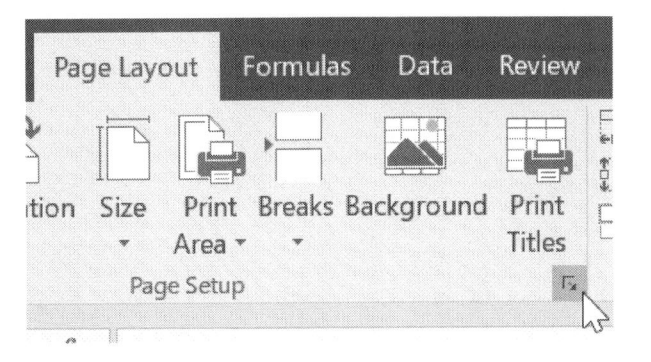

138- Select "Landscape", Fit to 1 page wide by 1 tall

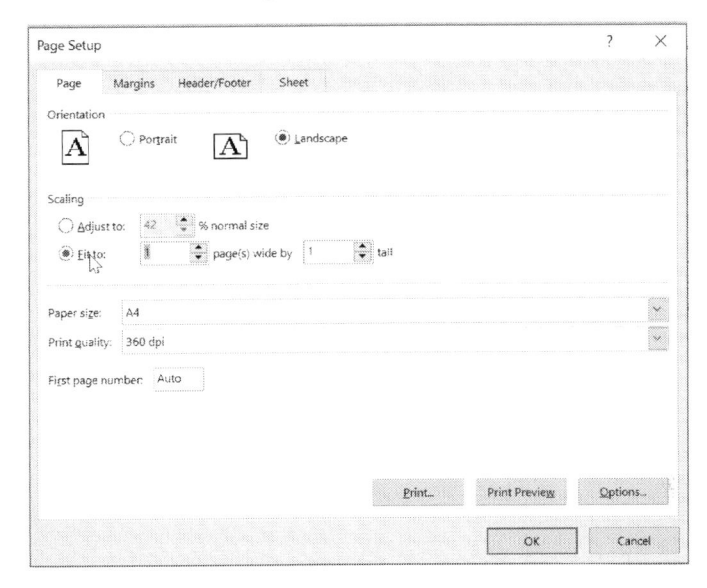

139- Go to "Margins" and check center on page "Horizontally" and "Vertically".

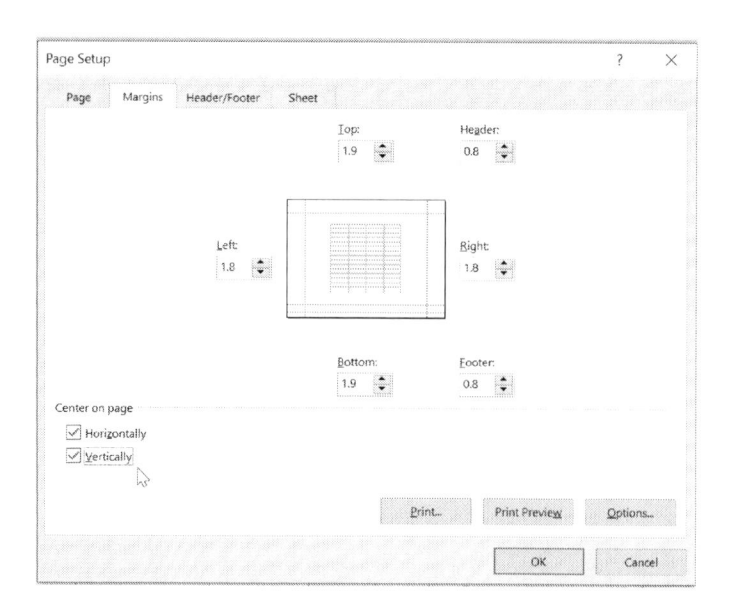

140- Go to "Header/Footer" and set the file name as "Header" and page as "Footer".

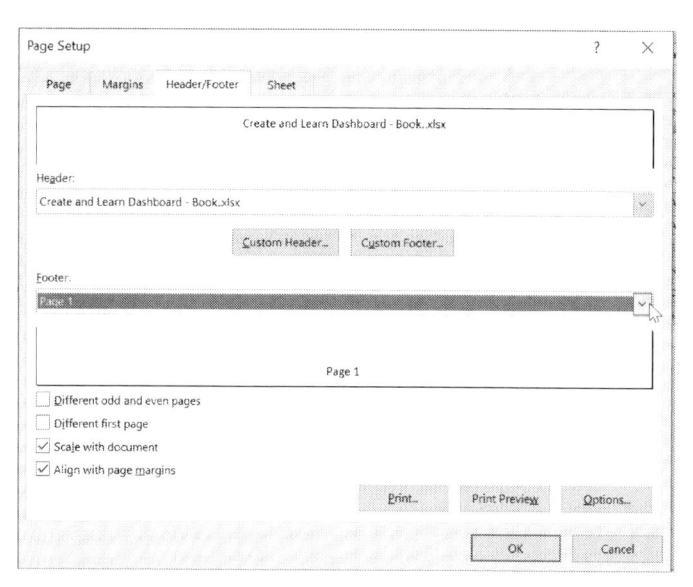

141- Go to "Sheet" and check if the print area is right. Then "OK".

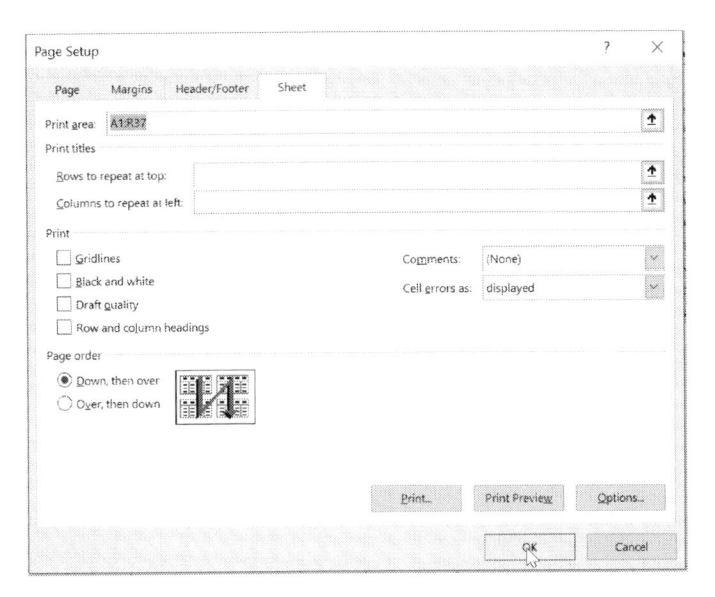

142- Go to "File" and select "Print".

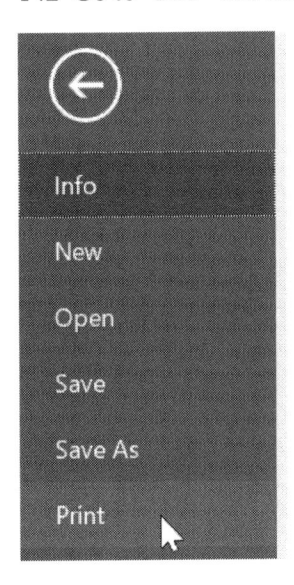

143- Check how your print would looks like, and click on "Save".

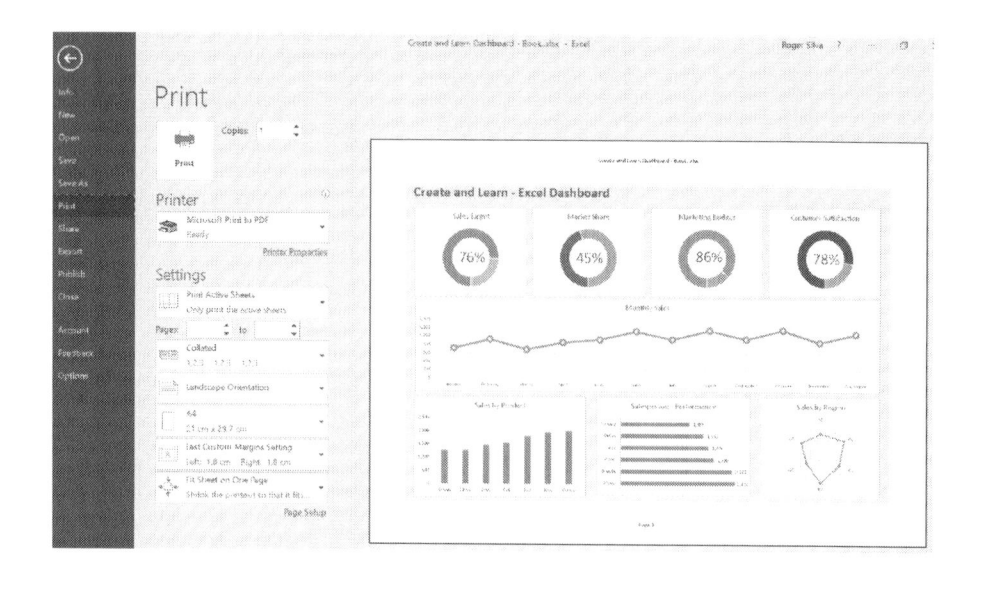

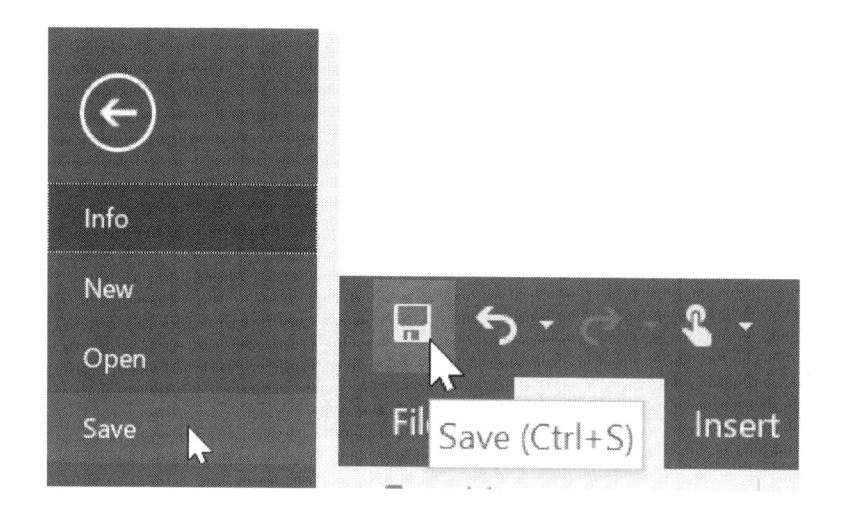

Congratulations! You have created a nice Dashboard using PivotTables, PivotCharts, Slicers, Timeline and more. Next chapter you will be able to change your dashboard.

9. Training tab

144- Select the entire sheet and copy.

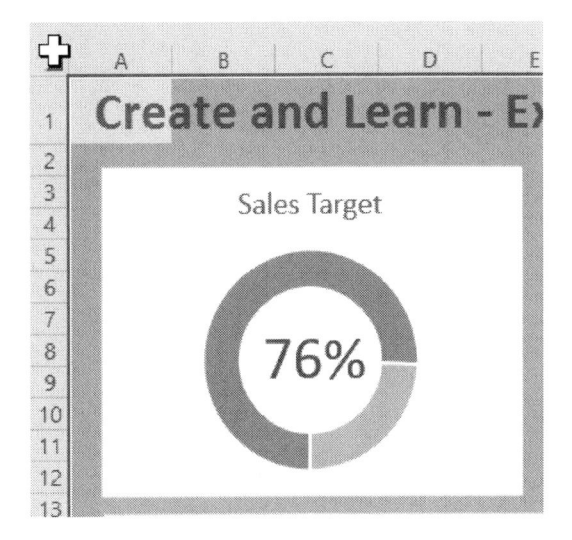

145- Go to "Training" sheet, select cell A1 and paste what you have copied.

146- Go to "Shapes" and insert a "Star".

147- Set the "Star" size as 0.5cm. Select the "Start" and copy.

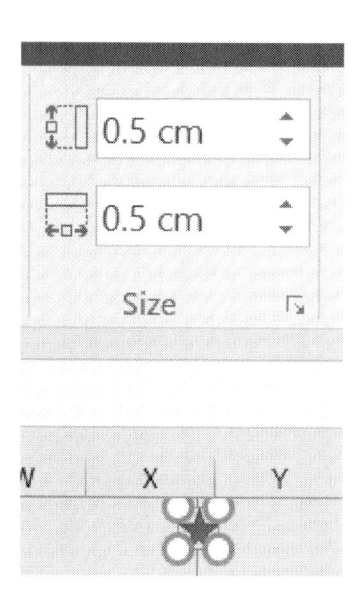

148- Select the "Series" on "Monthly Sales" chart and paste the "Star".

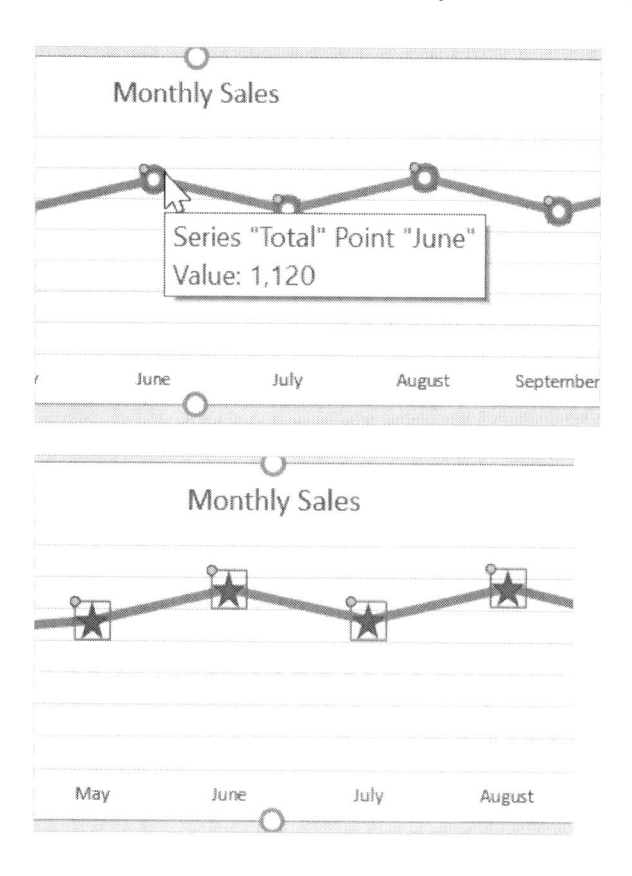

149- Go to "Format tab", "Shape Outline" and select "No Outline".

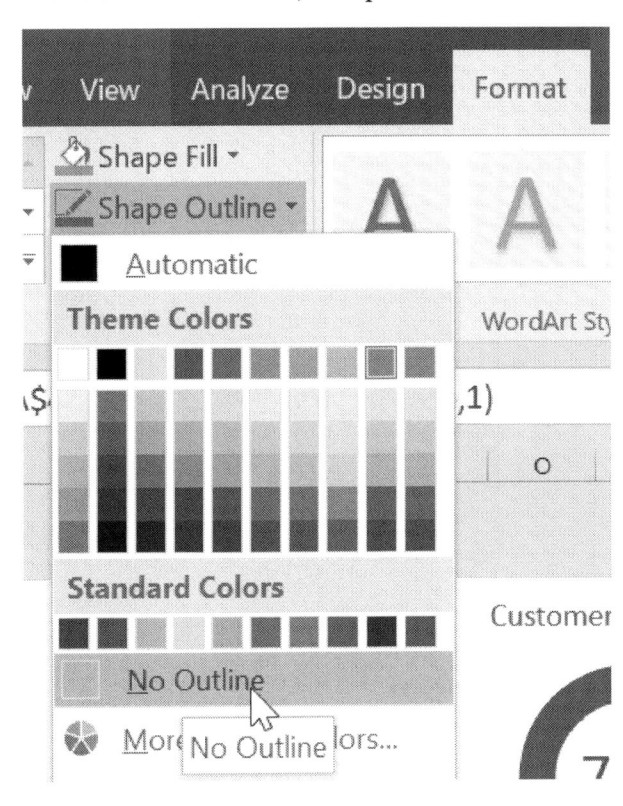

Go to "Chart Elements" and check "Data labels".

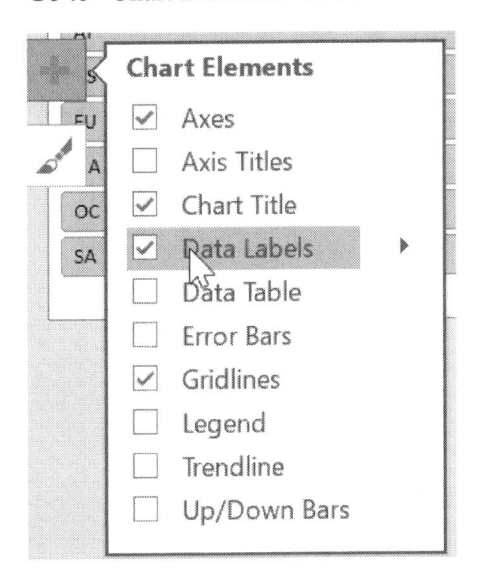

Select the Doughnut chart and go to "Design tab" and click on "Change Chart Type"

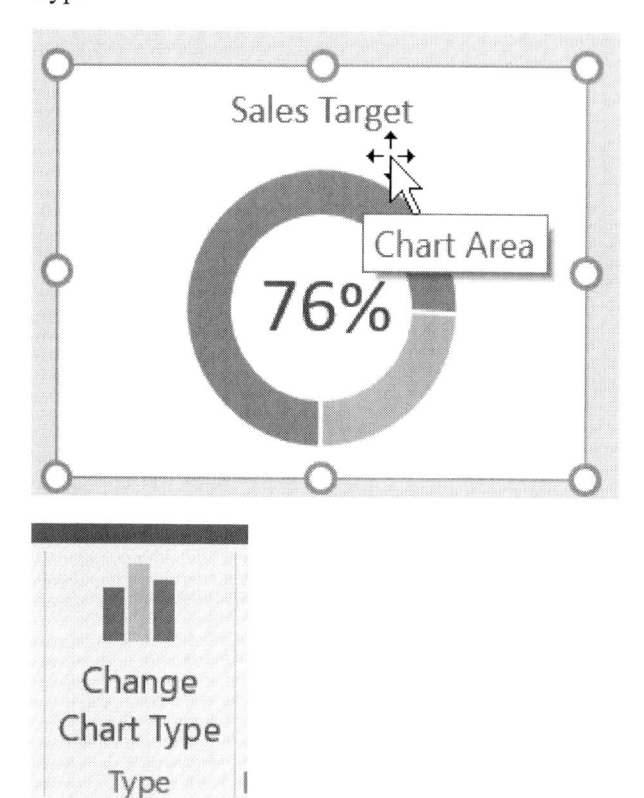

Select "Pie Chart" and move the text box to the corner and "Align Right".

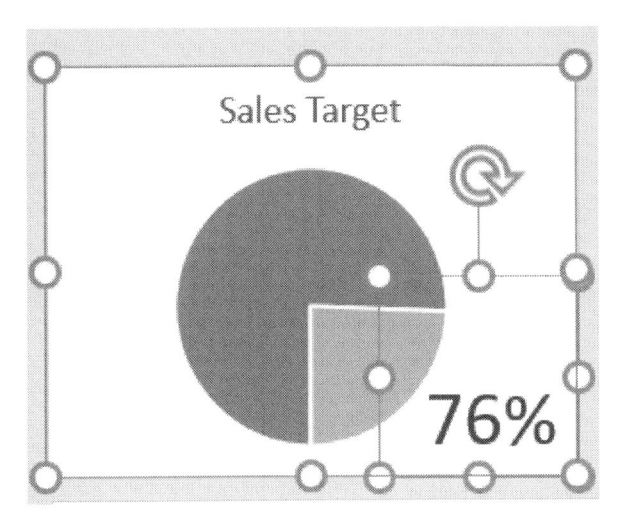

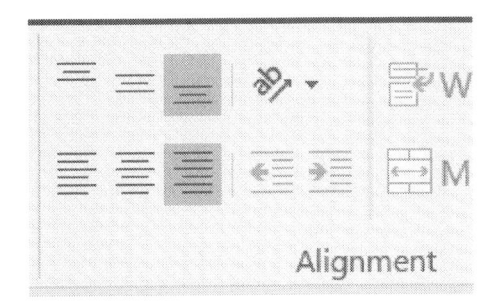

Change the charts type and filter styles to have a result like the image below.

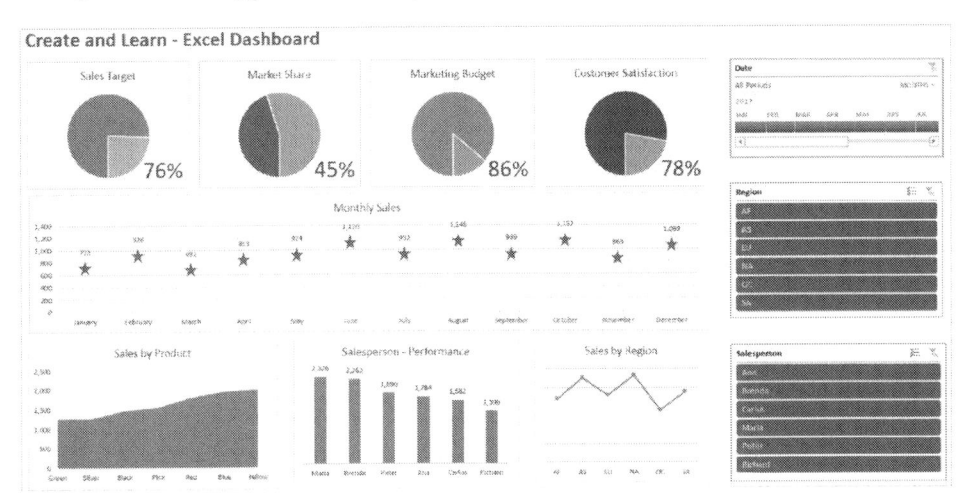

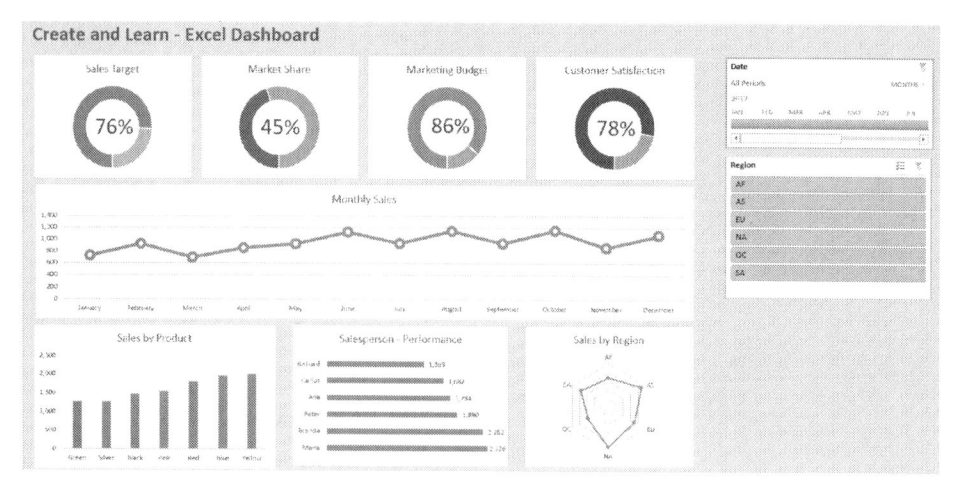

Dear reader.

A good rating and your positive review are incredibly important for me! If you have any comments or suggestion, please send me an email, or a message on LinkedIn and I will be more than happy to hear from you.

I hope you have achieved your goal to learn more about Microsoft Excel quickly and creating a beautiful and useful tool.

For its constant evolution, try my other books in the Create and Learn series and go evolving rapidly, create new tools and learn new practices in Microsoft Excel.

Thank you for the time we spent Creating and Learning.

Roger F. Silva

rogerfsilva1@gmail.com

You can find more Create and Learn books at http://rogerfsilva.blogspot.com

Printed in Great Britain
by Amazon